DAYS go by, not LOVE

Therese Benedict

Therese Benedict

DAYS go by, not LOVE

A Beautiful Journey of Change

Book 1

The Beginning of Your Journey

Sally keep your chin up and your memories deep in your heart.
love Betty

TATE PUBLISHING & *Enterprises*

Days Go By, Not Love
Copyright © 2010 by Therese Benedict. All rights reserved.

No part of this publication may be reproduced, stored in a retrieval system or transmitted in any way by any means, electronic, mechanical, photocopy, recording or otherwise without the prior permission of the author except as provided by USA copyright law.

This book is designed to provide accurate and authoritative information with regard to the subject matter covered. This information is given with the understanding that neither the author nor Tate Publishing, LLC is engaged in rendering legal, professional advice. Since the details of your situation are fact dependent, you should additionally seek the services of a competent professional.

The opinions expressed by the author are not necessarily those of Tate Publishing, LLC.

Published by Tate Publishing & Enterprises, LLC
127 E. Trade Center Terrace | Mustang, Oklahoma 73064 USA
1.888.361.9473 | www.tatepublishing.com

Tate Publishing is committed to excellence in the publishing industry. The company reflects the philosophy established by the founders, based on Psalm 68:11,
"The Lord gave the word and great was the company of those who published it."

Book design copyright © 2010 by Tate Publishing, LLC. All rights reserved.
Front Cover Photography & Bio Photo by Bruce Talbot (www.brucetalbot.com)
Manuscript Production/Design by Rik Boberg (www.monroe68.com)
Editorial by Jason F. Benedict
Cover design by Tyler Evans
Interior design by Jeff Fisher

Published in the United States of America

ISBN: 978-1-61566-832-8
1. Religion, Christian Life, Inspirational
2. Religion, Christian Life, Devotional
10.01.26

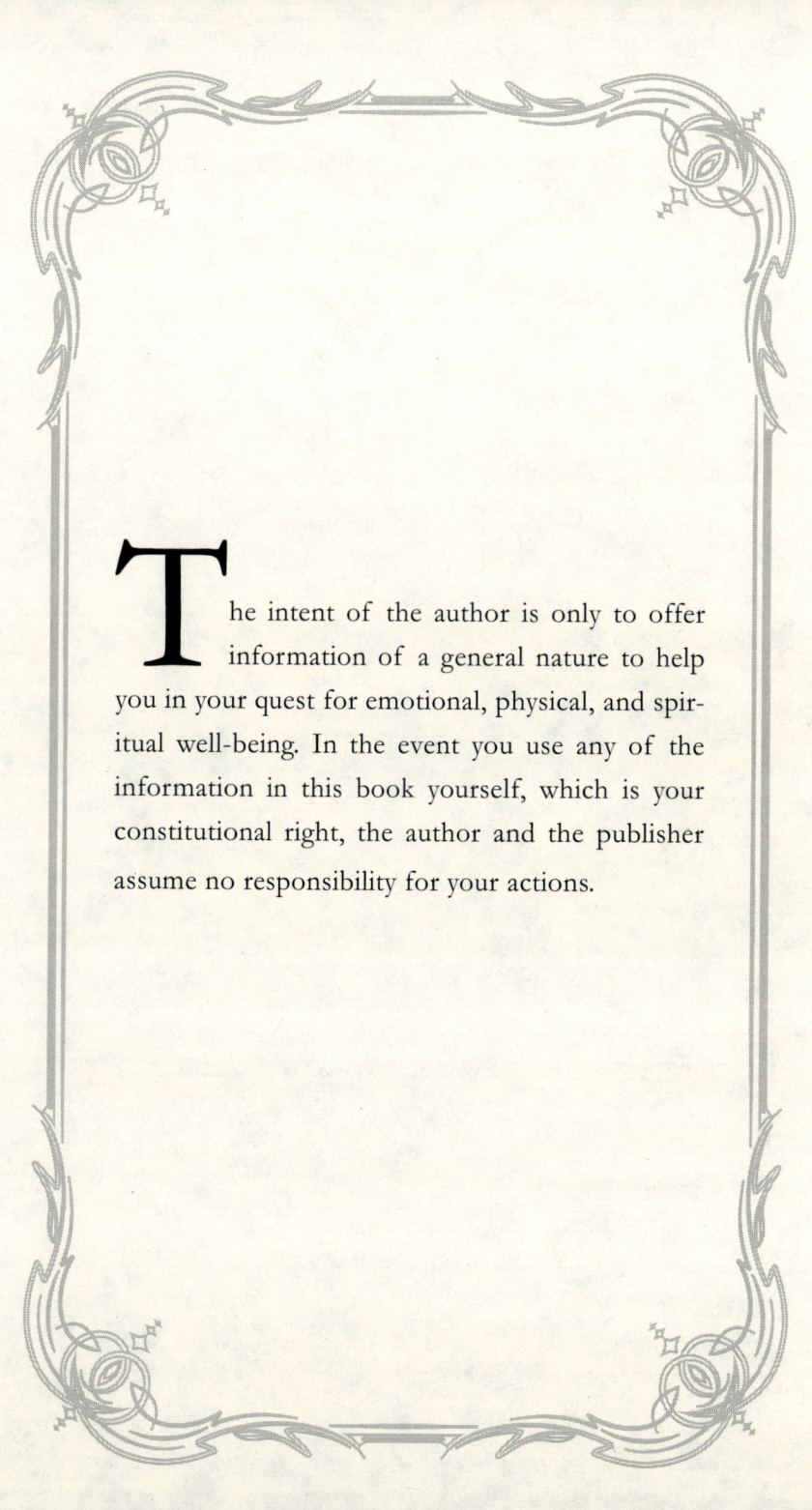

The intent of the author is only to offer information of a general nature to help you in your quest for emotional, physical, and spiritual well-being. In the event you use any of the information in this book yourself, which is your constitutional right, the author and the publisher assume no responsibility for your actions.

SPECIAL THANKS

I would like to give a special thank you to Rik Boberg, for his endless efforts on helping me with this book and for being there in a moment's notice from beginning to end. For being such a wonderful friend to Jason and I through this life changing experience; we will never forget your help.

I would also like to give a special thank you to Bruce Talbot, for taking the time out of his busy schedule for my photo shoot regarding my book and for his beautiful talent of photography ... which in turn made the cover of this book priceless with beauty.

TABLE OF CONTENTS

Dedication	11
Foreword	13
Introduction	15
Part I: **The Beginning**	21
Part II: **Self Acceptance**	43
Part III: **Healing**	69
Part IV: **Learning**	93
Part V: **Changes**	115
Part VI: **Actions**	139
Part VII: **Addictions**	159
Part VIII: **Messages**	181
Part IX: **Journeys**	201
Part X : **Making A Choice**	223
Letter from the Editor	247
Author's Note	251
About the Author	253

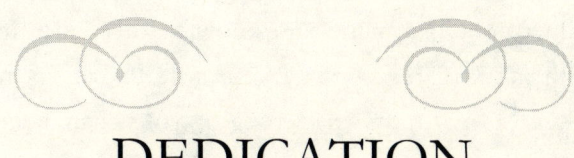

DEDICATION

To God, for loving me the way you love me and standing by my side while I help this world find peace in their souls. To my daughter, Valerie, for loving my life and standing by my side in what I need to do for others. You have given me unconditional love that I will cherish forever. You are such beauty of love, and I am proud to call myself your mother. To my daughter, Sara, for loving me so much and knowing how much I truly love you with the appreciation of you taking care of our home; for telling me how much you miss me, and loving your sister and brother so much. You are my precious moments. To my son, Branden, for showing me how much you love me by wanting me to be with you and your family; by telling me you miss me, calling me all the time, and most of all, telling me you love me every time we speak. For letting me help your relationship and knowing that I do this with my love for you and your wife to be. To my sister, Mary, for staying strong of your change and believing in the angels as you do. For taking care of me and my family with your generosity, love, and even through the hardest steps of your journey. To my husband, Jason, for loving me with great intense love, while holding my hand through my hard teachings. For holding me while I cried for the hurt that is being caused in this life here on earth. Thank you for being a part of helping this world and standing by my side protecting me from cruelty.

FOREWORD

*D*ays Go By, Not Love is not intended to be part of any competition, but rather to help progress the spiritual, religious, and self-help movement; a movement that defies separation and unifies love through choice. This book has been written from the words of God, and it is now time for his words to reach all of his children; to bring this world together instead of apart.

This book is written to all who wish to and are willing to try to change their life. This book can help parents be better parents, can help teachers to be better teachers, to help all overcome their anger, pain, and blindness to their hurt from their past and present actions of wrong and misunderstanding of life. It is important that we all know that we can get past our pain and why we are venting out to others who have not caused our pain. This book reaches out to anyone who needs to heal and to move forward with a life of love and peace. This book helps to bring eternal happiness from within and not just externally in our lives.

We recommend that as you begin your journey, that you write your feelings, thoughts, and emotions in the journal pages provided after each part of the book as you continue reading. This is very effective when used on a daily or weekly basis and vital to your growth of learning. This book is truly a road map of your journey and self-growth, therefore it is important that you do not lend this book out to your friends and/or family, we encourage you to buy them a copy as a gift for them to keep, enjoy and begin their own journey with God and his angels. God bless.

INTRODUCTION

I have walked the many emotions of life to help people heal from their past and present. I have walked with happiness of helping them find comfort and walked with sadness from the hurt that has crossed their paths. I have stated in my book, *Days Go By, Not Love* "When changing your life, it involves difficult times and it's not easy to change one's life. It is hard at times and by saying this to you, I mean, it is hard."

I have helped people with their life changes and I have walked through their pain with them. I have felt their pain and I have lived their pain. And I, myself, have felt the hurt rush through my soul with the ultimate of pain—not wanting to allow the feeling of destruction run through my body while tearing it up, but necessary to help heal others. I'm sure you know what I am saying, for many of you have felt this pain or are enduring and seeking guidance as you read this book.

I understand the pain that is out there in this world. However, when you help someone with the changes of their life for their purpose, you endure the pain, no matter how devastating it is or how long it takes. It's disturbing how one's life can be so happy, until the outer world walks in to demolish what happiness you have from within your life. Yet, you learn to keep walking on your journey no matter what it takes, to change you, your life, and to heal from your wounds. During this time, you trust in God and his angels. You learn how to speak with them for their comfort and guidance, so when you reach another situation, it is still difficult, but you see peace in your future.

The more you walk on your journey, the more you will understand when you give your life to God to change your wrong to right; there will always be a beautiful outcome. The journey itself changes who you are and what you see in this world. It brings discouragement and hardship, seeing how much negativity lies across this life we live. It teaches how you need to learn not to let negativity win and let the outer world stay outside, so you may keep your happiness of love and peace within. You learn to unlearn your wrong and turn them to right and to better who you are and become who you are meant to be. This book entails views of life in every direction. It is a wonderful experience; however, it will teach you strength at the same time.

Trust in your steps of change, for your happiness is waiting for you.

Part One

THE BEGINNING

Y ou will learn a journey of endless miles begins beneath one's feet and that the hardest part of a journey is to keep walking. A journey can take the physical form of a walk and turn into a spiritual transformation to enlightenment. Whichever the form of your journey (physical or spiritual), it will be a matter of learning and discoveries within your changes and progress from one stage to another. This enlightenment will show the inner-self a divine purpose and enchantment for life. Though you may not know what to expect, you can easily understand why they can become so inspiring and beautiful after just a few steps.

During your walk, you'll see you in all ways (mind, body, and soul). It might not be pretty to face; however, face what you need to change. Go inside your soul and see who you are and do not turn your head; for this may be a point you wish to stop walking. The messages you receive when walking this journey will be vivid and timely. Time is everything when you give your destiny to God and his angels. Time is your best friend, even though it may feel like an enemy. When time feels like your enemy, make time your friend by affirming your trust in God and the reasons for your change.

To complete this task, change what you are thinking. Seek the positive and release the wrong, for the signs of change will become clear. Face yourself, and don't stop walking. Facing yourself will bring about this change a in a timely manner. Release the blindfold and shower the unconditional love that waits to be given and received from those around you. So, while you walk this journey reintroduce yourself to the person you truly are inside. Let your inner voice shine with love over the outer complications in life. Change the wrong to right and feel the brightness from within.

On this journey, you will feel a deep awakening inside because you will begin to understand the hurt and pain that walks this earth. Painful situations will begin to occur, so you can see what you need to change from within and around. You will also build your trust and belief that God's angels know what they are doing and that they are there standing by your side. Your angels do not hurt you. They are there to protect you at all times. You may not feel that way when you are dealing with a difficult moment; however, you need to remember that it's for a reason, even if you don't understand what the reason may be.

When you give your life to God knowing your angels will help you complete your change in life— you will be successful in your heart's desires. You will learn how they speak to you, and how to make it through this life of positive change. It is important to trust what you are doing. To know you are making the right choice to better who you are as a person. To take the wrong inside yourself and make it right can and will change your life. You will see and feel this change within you. Use your transformation as a healing tool to help others want to change their lives as well.

Inside every one of us, we have something (emotionally, physically and/or mentally) we may want to fix. The wish to change this feeling can be many times over, for the fact we don't know how to complete this change that we hold inside us. That is when one gives up and just goes with the saying, "This is who I am." We once again hold inside us the bad we hate so much.

We all have bad habits that we want to break; cruelty, talking back (to win an argument), slamming doors, hitting and running away from what we've caused. The list can be endless; however, you know yours. We know what we want; we just do not know how to get it. We become lost within ourselves because we are stuck on how to change rather than accepting this transition. After confusion sets in, and takes something that seems so simple and makes it difficult, we learn that it's not an easy task. No matter how little or hard we try, our bad habits just won't go away on their own. So issues that surround these habits have to arise in order for us to grow and continue this unforeseen journey.

Learning to speak to your angels through your soul, thoughts, feelings, verbal affirmations, and/or physical actions can bring much comfort, especially when you're in fear or doubt. Speak to them knowing that they are there, not thinking that they are there. Believe in them, giving them your fears, worries, and your life. Speak to them, and then look for their answers. The answers come in many different ways: miracles or happenings that make a problem disappear, objects moving from one place to another, electricity flickering, and numbers that are seen over and over.

Learn how the angels speak to you by reading books, researching, watching TV specials about holy or angelic encounters; and pay attention to your spiritual intuition as well as your surroundings, and the messages that the angels are relaying to you will become clear. Practice everything you learn and use it with your heart. There are times that it may seem like everything is falling apart and there is no way of stopping this from happening, but this is where trust falls into place.

Give yourself to the angels; you will see miracles when this is in place. This life is an unbelievable one; however, it is also a world of pain and hurt because of the evil that walks this planet. There is so much worry that we carry within us that comfort is needed to keep us walking. Getting to know this life and accepting the transition ahead can and will be very confusing at times. However, the more trust you give the better your life becomes. Trust God, believe in his angels and believe in yourself. There are many different steps in walking this journey. Think of this as climbing a staircase, where you can only move upward. Some steps are easier than others, just keep taking them. Angels are not here to hurt you or lead you in the wrong direction. Angels are only here to help you. Knowing and understanding this will bring comfort while walking on your journey.

Since the time of our birth to our death, we have many angels surrounding us at all times. Angels are never to leave you, for they are here protecting you from the evil that walks among us. When you are conscious of this understanding and you want to change your life, is when you will truly see that angels are with you. I cannot stress enough to trust them to help you. I have lived this life since I was born and have seen many miracles.

Catastrophic events and miracles take place every day. Not to drag you through the mud, but to better your understanding of the angels and their messages. In relationships, it can become frustrating, because you are learning how to love. In many relationships, we walk around stating the words, "I love you," and doing nothing to show that love. We need to learn how to love and express love by actions. You might think, *I do show love;* however, your way of showing love is not enough.

Understanding your loved one is the most difficult part of a relationship; however, when you understand your partner, you will know what they need in your actions of love. This will be discussed throughout the book and will be an eye opener for those struggling in relationships and how to show love with actions in any direction of the relationship.

Remember, there are many relationships in your life, through family, friends, and even within yourself. And each relationship encounters different situations to consider on your journey. Knowing this journey starts with yourself and stems in all directions of your life, can help you learn how to apply them in every direction and not just from within. Take this journey by starting from within and then begin focusing on any aspect of your life. An aspect can be any part or a whole of your life that you choose to focus on. The more you learn about your true self while walking with honesty on this journey, the more it will make sense. It all connects within a divine network of your spiritual growth.

Who that walks in honesty will walk a life of truth. Not an easy life at first; however, you will adjust to walking a life of right.

Guidelines to Journaling:

The following pages provided are to help you keep track of your goals, struggles, accomplishments and what you need to change about yourself. Remember to be very honest with yourself. Write down what you would like to work on, how you worked on it and where your struggle came about (if you had any), then you can write down what you have accomplished with what changes you are trying to make. This is very effective when used on a daily or weekly basis and vital to your growth of learning.

Accomplishments Regarding Part One

Accomplishments Regarding Part One

Accomplishments Regarding Part One

Accomplishments Regarding Part One

Accomplishments Regarding Part One

Accomplishments Regarding Part One

Accomplishments Regarding Part One

Accomplishments Regarding Part One

Accomplishments Regarding Part One

Accomplishments Regarding Part One

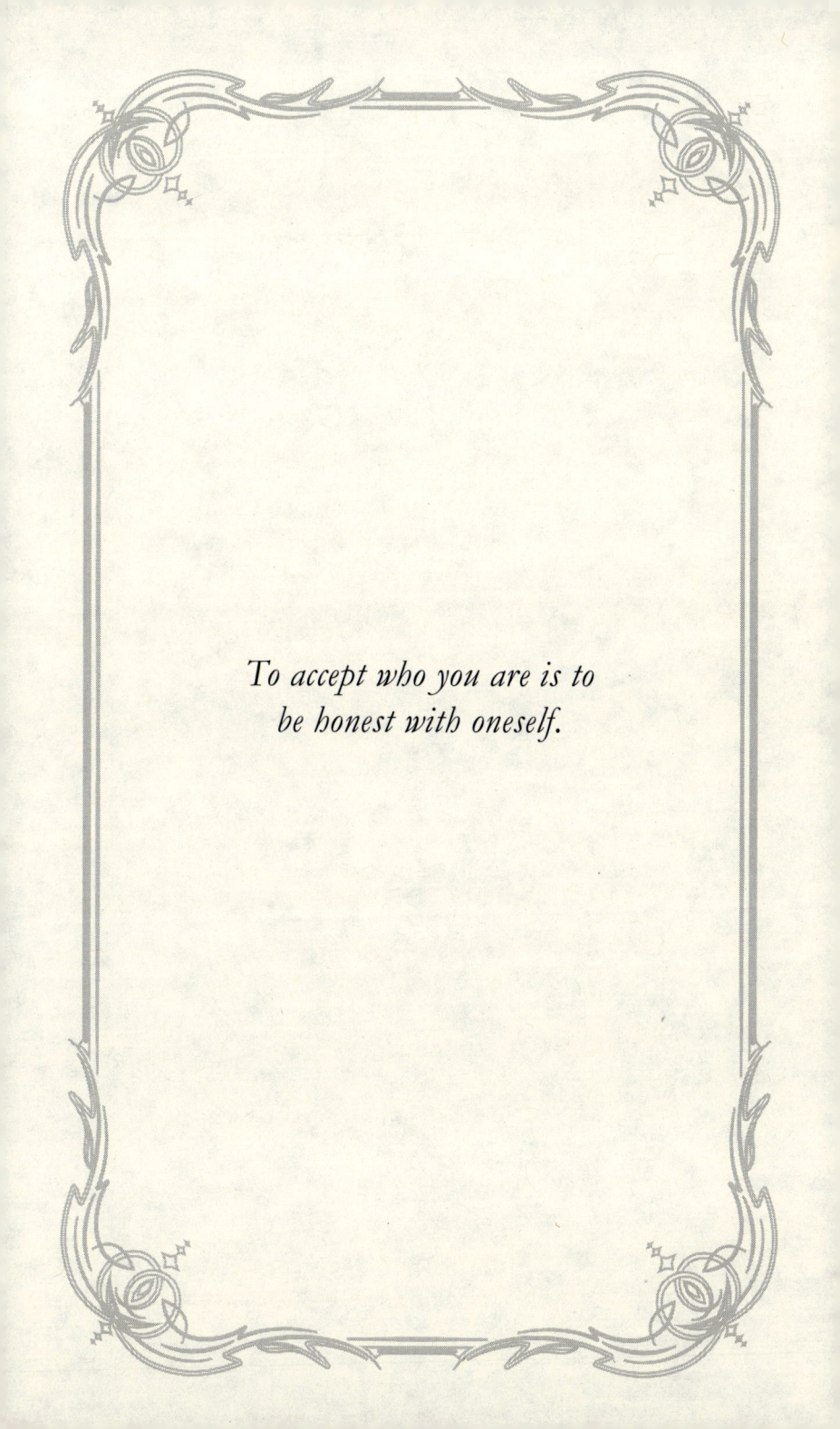

To accept who you are is to be honest with oneself.

Part Two

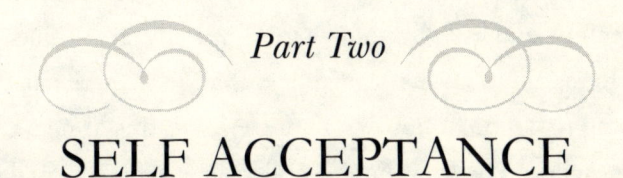

SELF ACCEPTANCE

Now let's start with acknowledging yourself; to see the inner you and to face your strengths and weaknesses. Do not think of this as a painful process. Look at this as a wonderful experience, knowing you are going to take a beautiful but hard journey of who you are and who you are going to become. Do this with happiness in your soul. Think of yourself as being reborn and taking your first breath and new steps to living with your soul and not your mind. Sure, you're going to fall, get a few bumps and bruises along the way, but the important thing is to get back up and continue walking. When you do this, you won't believe the miracles you will see and be in disbelief of the ones you've missed all along; when you walk the journey you are about to take.

Start by sitting down with yourself. Clear your mind, and think about who you really are inside. Remember, it's just you and your angels you're talking to, so be honest with yourself. Do this at night, when you're lying in bed and your eyes are closed resting with visions of change. Look deep inside your soul and get to know who really exists inside. Do this every night until your visions of change become visions of reality. We all have good intentions inside, but if they only exist in our minds, that's all they ever become: visions. Think of the good you have inside and then think of how often you use it.

When you bring out the good from within; do you bring it out all the time, sometimes or just when you feel like it? Do you bring it out when you're in a good mood or even when you're not? You will learn that when you bring out the good in every second of your life; you're doing everything in your power to be who you really are inside. When you're having a hard moment, stop and apply your good to what could become a negative situation. When you do this you will see the blessings the angels bring to you. Never give up on the good that lies within, because of the hardships of life. Do not let the worst come out of you and take it out on the world and the people that come across your path. Never stop trying or let this world take you away from true inner strength. This is when you use your inner strength to your fullest. When you come across someone who is having a bad day, try to make their day a little better, instead of them making your day a little worse. Practice this every day and see what good can bring to people you know and don't know. You will feel wonderful by making someone's day a little better. When we continue bringing the good out, we see more of the innate spirit shine through instead of being hidden away. Do not hide this beautiful gift. Share this good with others and watch the seed you've planted grow within the hearts of many.

When you practice bringing out your good, it strengthens your weakness. It helps you see more of the weakness inside of you, which can help you progress your transition toward seeking the positives and building your weakness to become your strength. Do not let someone's weakness take away your strength. Use your strength to make understanding come into play. Understanding can be painful to practice, but also comforting to you and those around you. Understanding, is a key element to getting through hardships and to help you see what you need to change in yourself, which in turn will help change your life, one step at a time.

You will learn more of why you dwell on your weaknesses, through understanding and how it can give strength to make other positive changes as your journey progresses. Understanding, helps you see more of the inner you, which sometimes we forget even exists. You will start receiving answers to questions you did not know you even had. When this begins to happen and you face your challenges, whether good or bad—do not look away and stop walking; for your journey has already begun. Keep moving forward in everyway to become a better you. Do not forget to talk to your angels and seek their divine guidance while walking your journey.

You need to learn to understand yourself before you can try to understand others. Plus, it is a good way to practice understanding. In this process you see more of yourself, which helps you to learn more about others. It helps you understand that there are reasons for other people's personalities and the rationale behind your surroundings. There are reasons for who we are and who we have become. This also helps on blocking negative judgment to and from others. We all need to understand that we do not ask for our past as a child; however, neither did our parents. Not saying that we all had a terrible past, but we all have had something that has affected our lives; including the experiences that we have endured with our growth.

Now, this is where we learn not to judge others, but to understand oneself. Why do we have so much anger inside of ourselves? We hold anger from the past and anger toward the present. Some of us tend to hold anger inside because we do not understand why we were hurt and were treated wrong. Maybe it was because of our actions toward others, or it was a lesson being taught by God or our angles that we didn't quite understand. Sure, we may have deserved a taste of our own medicine, but remember, we can easily take a situation wrong because of our past wrong doings or because of a past hurt the other person was enduring that was unknown to us. It is a terrible cycle that can stem from one misunderstanding or misjudgment and lead to a ripple effect that affects many around us. All of this really has to do with more understanding of why we are who we are. When we learn about other people's past, it takes the pain away of "Why are they hurting me?" Learning that it is them in pain and not you is a comfort when recognized. Understanding oneself and others takes a different direction by realizing the anger subsides within others. This is confusing to understand; however, the confusion diminishes as your understanding of them becomes clearer. Time is again taking place during this entire journey.

Time will heal your heart and soul. For time is the only way to truly learn. As you walk this journey, remember you are not walking alone. Talk to your angels constantly and never think you're taking this journey by yourself. As you walk, you will begin feeling tired, because you are working on all aspects of you [mind, body, and soul] and practicing what you've learned on those around you. It's important to remember that the people you are practicing on may not have a positive response to your messages or actions. This is because you have a deeper understanding of yourself and truly speaking from your soul and they do not understand this for they do not speak from their soul. They hold the negative or selfishness inside themselves from their past and bring it to the present.

In time your true self begins to shine and your new life begins to blossom. Your family and friends will see you and will see the person they love is truly showing. They too will begin to understand and see your transition and begin to ask questions about how you can help them bring their true self to life. That's when you know you are helping this world bring back the love and kindness that God wills.

Make a difference by continuing to work on your change while healing others with theirs. Remember, this is only the beginning of your journey and that we have only begun to touch the surface of your transformation. You can see the beauty and hope of new love and passion for life; however, many hardships await you on this walk. You will learn that you cannot stop at any one of these steps. Try with all of you, not part of you, while walking this journey. Learn to love through every second of your day. Pray for help and strength from God and your angels every day and night. So you may love everyone as you truly are, so others may love you the same.

Loving yourself is most important on your journey. Being honest with yourself is being loving and respectful to your desired change. Remember, you are the one who can treat you the way you've always wanted to be treated. So with saying that, learn to be the first to treat yourself right. Do not forget that if you treat yourself wrong, you only hurt others more and slow the process of change. When you learn to be honest with yourself, you learn to be honest with others. Lies are and will always be hurtful to others as well as losing respect of others around you. Being honest shows people that there is a trust factor within you and that you realize you are hurting them. Not being honest loses the respect from others because of the hurt that stems from your lies.

Honesty is so important in your life, and understanding it has a great affect regarding your livelihood. When you are honest with yourself, you have a right to stand up in a situation instead of fighting for someone to believe your position. It is horrible to live your life in a manner of dishonesty. Be good to you, so you can be good to others. When you treat others right, you will not have to lie. Makes sense doesn't it? If not, you need to think about that question.

Think good and hard on this journey and it will help you strengthen your inner self. You will also learn that being honest will bring you a free life, instead of a captive one. As you walk this journey, you will see the relief and feel the freedom of this terrible habit. You will need at least a good six months to practice true honesty, so that you are strong to continue. This does not mean that it takes six months to accept this change. It just means that it takes this time to build an understanding of true honesty with it being conscious on your mind at all times. That way when you start falling back, you're aware that you're slipping and able to get back on track. The angels help you with this in many ways. This is another major reason why you want to learn the understanding of their messages. The angels do many things you might not understand until you learn what you are dealing with at that time. It will become clearer to you as your journey grows.

God and the angels work in mysterious ways. Miracles that you may have thought would never come true; appear before your eyes. However, beautiful and wonderful, they are learning tools. They will always come through for you. Sometimes you will wonder how, but you will learn that nothing is impossible for the angels. The hardest obstacles or challenges for people can be just as easy as the little ones for the angels to fix. The angels can do anything, no matter what it is. Hold their hands tightly if necessary and just keep walking.

Trust, faith, and belief are other important factors. Keep working on yourself with the angels and they will take care of you. On your journey, you will learn this is true with every step you take. Grow a personal relationship with your angels. You can talk to them about your most personal issues. You can speak to them with complete honesty about anything. You can learn this by acknowledging your deepest fears and about you, period. The beautiful result in doing this is that you can open up completely and you do not have to worry about others finding out your personal feelings or secrets. Remember to do this knowing your angels are there. Do not think, "I will give this a chance" by hoping they are standing by your side. Believe they are there and you will see the results. Sometimes the results can be immediate or take place over time. It truly depends on the situation at hand and the lesson that you are learning about with the angels. Sometimes, it is short-lived or it can take days. Either way, the outcome will always be the same: beautiful. When you are doing right, you will see the good that happens to you right away. And when you start going the opposite direction, they will show you you're going the wrong way by little situations that start happening around you. This will remind you you're not staying on track with your personal mission. These situations are a way the angels can speak to you when you're doing well and when you're beginning to fall off track. So don't take it personally when you fall, they do this to help you. Angels are from God and they only work with love.

When you live a life of happiness and are kind to others, you learn (on your journey) how to be there for others, to care about what other people go through; even when you don't know them. You learn to do acts of kindness and impact other people's lives, which will impact yours. When you learn this, you will feel from your soul that it is the right thing to do. At this point, you feel the brightness inside and this feeling is incredible. However, you will also start to see the sadness in this world; the cruelty, selfishness, and greed that is trying to take over the good. Everyone can help with bringing back the good in this life. But we all have to start with ourselves. There is so much on this earth that has faded away because people are protecting themselves from the harm that has spread in our lifetime. Their guards are up to shield the evil that walks this planet and we look at strangers with fear. We watch all around us, in fear, looking to make sure we don't get hurt. This is a sad surrounding that can be easily changed by trusting in God and your angels to help bring back the good that waits to shine within each of us.

The angels want the world to know they are here to help and that it is time for you to realize the spiritual life that lies dormant around you. Many of us do not believe in this life and have their own opinions regarding it. Some know this life, believe in it, but do not know how to live it. This information will help all who try. Once you make your change, your relationship changes with the angels. You have your personal relationship with them and you learn to trust them with all the good and bad in your life.

You know there are reasons that situations arise in your life and you know everything will be okay. You understand that if you do not know why something is happening at that time, you will in the end. This is a very comforting life to live and makes life easier and happier. The love, caring and understanding makes your life at peace. A lot of us do not know what peace feels like, so you will love the feeling even more. Peace is a feeling of calm, relaxation, and true happiness inside. Not dwelling on the negative happenings in your life. Peace is an inner-self feeling, not an external one. Peace is comforting—a bright aura inside that is a blessing for all who carry this gift.

Accomplishments Regarding Part Two

Accomplishments Regarding Part Two

Accomplishments Regarding Part Two

Accomplishments Regarding Part Two

Accomplishments Regarding Part Two

Accomplishments Regarding Part Two

Accomplishments Regarding Part Two

Accomplishments Regarding Part Two

Accomplishments Regarding Part Two

Accomplishments Regarding Part Two

*To heal one's soul, you
must take the first step.*

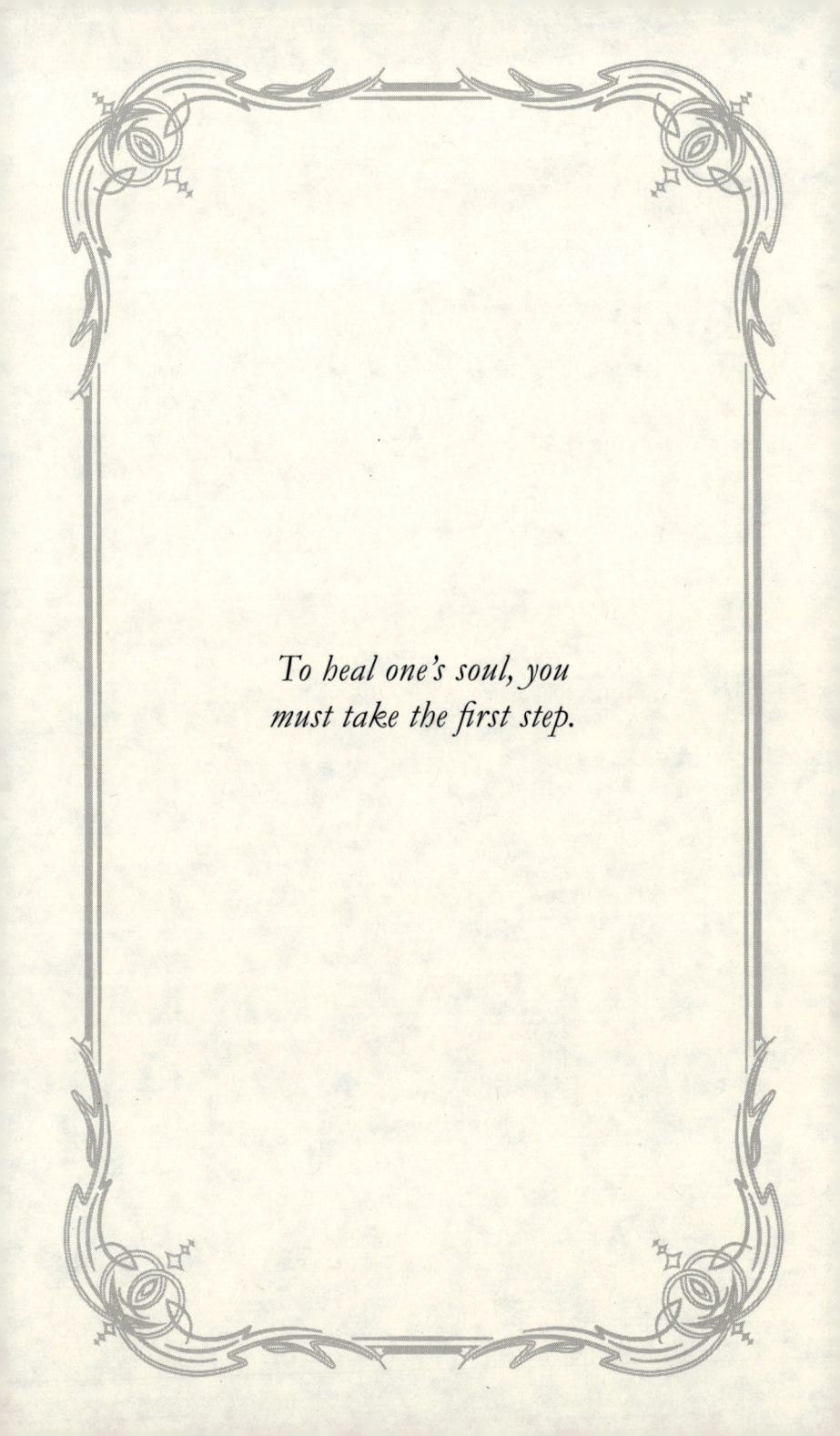

Part Three

HEALING

Now let's go back to the beginning, regarding lying in bed thinking of the inner you. You're lying there thinking of who you are right now. Think of the things you like about yourself first; the good. Think only on the good. Think about when you do the good, how often you do those actions of good and most importantly, why you do them. Remember, be honest; truly honest. It's between you and God. God already knows the truth, so you cannot hide anything even if you try. By doing this you learn to be more honest with yourself. God does not hold anything against you, so do not be embarrassed when mediating. God is happy you are making this change and he loves you no matter what mistakes we have made. Practice this thought until you know you are being honest with yourself. When you have been truly honest with yourself, then you take the next step.

Now, start thinking about what you don't like about yourself. When you do this be honest; remember it is between you and God. Think of the little things that you know you do wrong and most importantly, why you do them. Face the pain and the hurt and move on with why you have been expressing this negative side of you. Think about it often and heal from this hurt. Confront who you need to confront and ask yourself why you continue with this pain. Approach this with love, so you can receive an honest answer in return. Then move to each one of the findings of your dislikes, so you may heal from them and stop your negative behavior. Understanding why you behave negatively leads you to the core of your pain and will help you heal. Now, you may not get to all the answers, but knowing there are reasons for each helps lead you closer to the unanswered questions about your pain.

This can become very confusing because of the fact that we all have pain in our lives and it branches in so many directions. Remember, we all are going through something and we all carry issues of the past. So you need to understand that we take things in different ways, because we all have different opinions on relationships and life. Now, knowing this, ask yourself, *Do I need to confront everything or just the ones that matter?* Do not be so hard on yourself during this step. Know that this can become very confusing until you are further along on your journey. However, you need to acknowledge this step now and act on what you feel so you can move forward. Believe in yourself; do not just go by other people believing in you. Know that you are worth a value greater than defeat and continue your journey with belief. Believing in yourself is all you need, and use the belief of others as a support system. Focus on you and know you deserve this chance of a new beginning.

If you have a bad day, keep going and don't let that bad day be a reoccurring chain. Look at the day to see why and how it became a bad day. Was it something you started or did you let someone else start it for you? If it was either, know you have the power to reverse that day. During this process, you will learn to think at that moment and change your thoughts and reverse your reactions to that moment. As you walk this journey, you will start to see how your cocoon will soon blossom into a butterfly. Use this to keep you strong; you will want to give up many times along your journey because of the set backs of others and your wrong thinking. Embrace this change as it helps you regarding the effects of others' wrong doings that you come across. In doing so, you will learn to control the effects of others, when negative.

Take care of you and love yourself during this journey. Loving yourself the right way is not selfish. Let the angels remind you this is a wonderful act. When you love yourself for the right reasons, meaning you have the right to love you, as long as you are not hurting others in this process. Do not hurt people to get what you think you deserve or because you know that person loves you. Love seems to be fading in this world because of the unknown hurt or because of the hurt that follows. We are afraid of the unknown chances we face. When we fall victim to the fear we are walking in a relationship of disaster, which only poisons the relationship. Our minds think wrong because we think the worst. Then we accuse and then the turmoil begins. Think positive and manifest the outcomes you seek.

This cycle will not stop until we learn how to communicate with love and understanding of the people around us. Fear tends to take over us until it controls every ounce of freedom we have, instead of us controlling the fear. Learn about your friends, family or spouses past, so you can learn about their fears. When you learn about their past, you have a better understanding of why they do the things they do and why they take certain situations in their own way. By learning about your loved ones, friends, or even your parent's life, you have a better understanding and your relationship is on a better path. Your disagreements will make more sense and end more quickly. You will be more forgiving and you won't carry so much hurt. By truly and honestly getting to know the people in your life, you have a better understanding about them and it helps your life to be light-hearted and not so stubborn. If this does not make sense to you, try doing this and feel the experience, then you will understand this step.

When you do this step, it does not only help you, but them as well. When there is no understanding the hurt is deeper, and it is harder to forgive and you carry it within yourself longer than desired. By doing this you become more and more angry inside and the anger goes from one relationship to another. Getting to know yourself is important for you and your relationships and will benefit your life. You need to address this with strength and courage and trust everything, even when it does not look positive. The angels bring these situations up for the lessons of trusting, believing and know that everything will work out beautifully in the results of your efforts of this hardship. Again, time can be difficult to endure while facing these hardships; however, it will change your life forever.

Take this journey and embrace it with love and commitment. Get rid of the wrong and create more right. You will see your life change in so many different ways. You will understand everything around you in a better way. You will walk in an unblended light, instead of confusion. You will learn to love life the way it was meant to be loved: happily.

Take your steps to a better you and learn to love yourself with kindness. Get rid of your cruelty, so you may receive less in return. Take away your cold and replace it with warmth. Put more love inside and push away the hate. Learn to give without wanting something back. Take the time to listen without getting up and turning away. Try to understand without placing blame or wrong onto others. Make life wonderful and not miserable. Love others as you have always wanted to be loved.

Now, change your life to your dreams and let time lead the way; for time is everything. You will learn that time is hard to endure, but do not be stubborn with yourself, give yourself this chance. Do not ignore what you need to face, for you will only take more time away from the healing. Trust in you, for you are the key to success. Do this test of life and be all you can be to yourself and those around you. It sounds simple; however, it is far from simple. Just take one step at a time and do those steps at your pace, since you are doing this for yourself.

Read books about love, understanding, trust, and/or the angels or the spiritual realm to seek guidance. Speak to any kind of positive counsel or research books about inspiring stories—there are a lot of good ones out there. Write down your thoughts and experiences about your journey from day one and the findings that you are learning of your inner-self. Try not to miss a day, and do everything to make the time for your entry at the end of the day. This is also a good way to meditate, reflect on your day, and talk with God and your angels. Do not read your journal until after one month, and then repeat from the beginning after each month, to see how far you have walked in the positive light. It becomes a beautiful story of your life, when holding nothing back in your writing and expressing everything you are going through and feeling. After six months, you will see how sublime you have become.

Remember, the angels are with you every step of the way; never forget this thought. Turn your head and speak to them for they hear every word and know every emotion. They understand your struggles on your journey before you even experience them. They know your anger and understand why. They know your weaknesses and know how to make them strengths. They know your pain, the hurt you carry, and they want to help you heal from them. They also know how to accomplish taking them away.

Walk with your angels, speak to them, and believe in them. Trust them with everything: your thoughts, actions, wrong doings, your good, and all your relationships. Watch how they change your life even if you do not understand what they do. When you wonder why it is not getting better in a relationship, you need to remember the lesson was not meant for you, but for them. Learn to open your mind and think spiritually. Broaden your thoughts in every direction. When learning to do this, you will find that you mostly think negative and not positive. You need to think of the positive and look for the positive when faced with the negative. There are reasons for everything that comes across your path. Remember, you may not understand why until the situation is over. Look back at the situation to see what obstacles you came across and the reasoning behind them. You will get better at understanding the messages along your journey, just keep walking.

When you start this journey and you feel that you want to give up with the angels; the angels will not let you give up. They will push you to keep going, because you are struggling with your change and will show you with their messages to not give up. We all need encouragement to keep walking. The angels do this out of love, so that you do not give up. What people do not understand is that the angels do this for you every day, you just don't realize it because you're living your everyday life and walking through the hardships. You bypass all their messages because you are not living this spiritual life. You do not realize that angels are everywhere and everyone has them in their lives. Learn to speak to them for guidance and help; to understand their messages. Start your day by talking with them and end your day in the same way. By doing this, it gives you strength, courage, and hope for your day. Please, trust in them. Life is full of unnecessary hurt. Some of that hurt we cause ourselves, and some is caused by others' actions.

There is so much pain that scours this earth and demeans our way of life. All of us can help change this chain of misery. We can do this by starting with ourselves. Work from the inside out. Start within and then help others. Show them that life is happy when it comes from within. What you do for your life and what the meaning of life means to you, no matter how hard life gets, you have to keep living it. So why not live it in peace? You feel the peace more and more as time goes by. Feel the peace and share it with all acts of kindness and love for who you are becoming. Let this life be what God meant it to be. God wants this journey to be a wonderful experience, not a tragic one; learn the meanings of his words, to understand all senses of love and one sense of love. Learn of him and his angels so you can learn how they protect you through your life here on earth. Life is a gift, not a punishment. So take this gift and make it the best present you have ever received.

Do not wish harm on anyone. Ask God to teach those around us who are doing wrong. Help them see the hurt they are causing, not just to you, but for the fact that if they are hurting you, they are more than likely hurting others too. Pray that they see this message out of love, not anger. In a lot of cases it needs to get worse for them to see, before it gets better. Walk through this with strength and understanding and know that you are helping them to become a better person. Hold the angels' hands as tight as you need too. Believe me; they can take your strength. Angels love when you call upon them; they do not get tired and can be in more than one place at a time. They want you to call on them; that is why they are here, to help you in your life. Take their help. We all need help in some way or another in our lives. They want this world to know more about them and why they are here. They want to provide us comfort in our times of need. Talk to them not only to help you, but also to help others in need. Pray to God with everything and love him as he loves you. Be grateful he is our Father and learn to trust him, for he has trust in you. Walk with him, for he walks with you.

Accomplishments Regarding Part Three

Accomplishments Regarding Part Three

Accomplishments Regarding Part Three

Accomplishments Regarding Part Three

Accomplishments Regarding Part Three

Accomplishments Regarding Part Three

Accomplishments Regarding Part Three

Accomplishments Regarding Part Three

Accomplishments Regarding Part Three

Accomplishments Regarding Part Three

_____

_____

_____

_____

_____

_____

_____

_____

_____

_____

_____

_____

_____

_____

To learn is to listen.

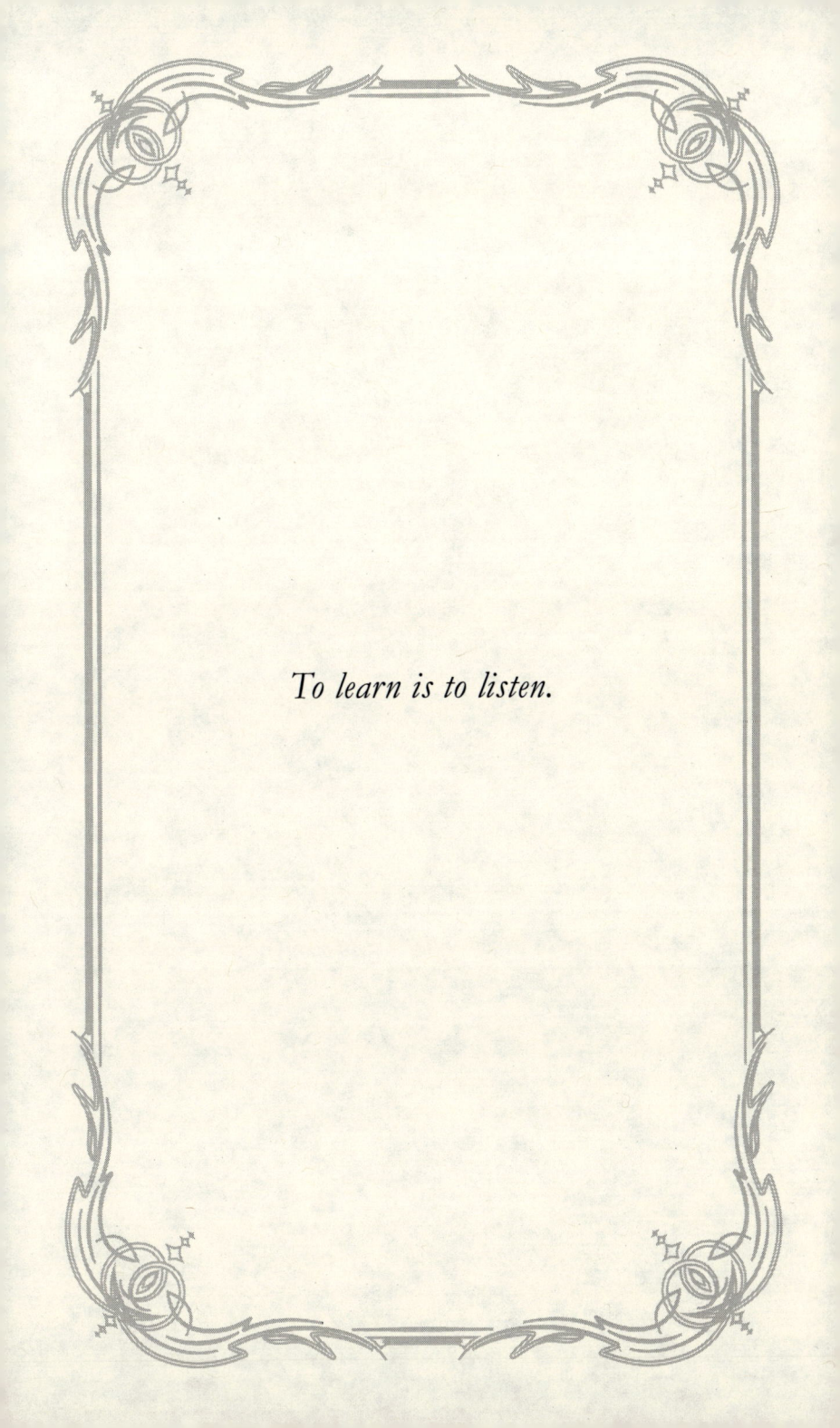

Part Four

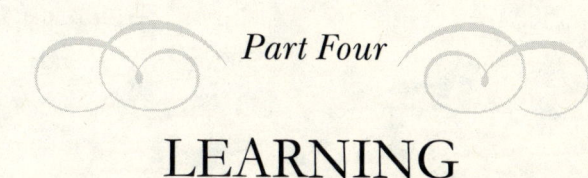

LEARNING

Whether harsh, soft, sarcastic, or just plain rude, the way you speak and the tone inflections used is a major cause of confusion and determinant of others' reactions. We need to learn to speak with our hearts and leave out the cruelty. It will allow others to listen and not react in a defensive manner. You will learn, by doing this, that you will be heard more often than not. It is hard for someone to react with anger when they understand you are speaking from the heart. When you speak from your heart, your heart radiates passion and your inner voice speaks universally to others. When this happens, your feelings are being considered and others understand more of the wrong they are doing to you and to others.

Having a conscious mind enables one to stop expressing hurt and allows us to have a better understanding for other peoples' feelings. The more cautious we are of how we treat others will provide a common ground for trust and open communication, just by expressing yourself in the right way. It is hard to speak the right way when you hurt inside, but you have to remember to speak with the love from within, so that you can speak appropriately.

When you speak in anger, it brings fear to others and you get the wrong reaction rather than the one you want to receive. Know that when you speak right, you will most likely get the right response with loving emotions attached. Then they will have the understanding you are trying to get across. They will hear you with your heart and not your anger, which is a much easier way for them to listen. Everything you do matters to what you want to accomplish. When you speak with your soul, others listen with theirs. When you speak with anger, you get anger back. When you speak soft, you receive a soft response. When you express with compassion, you receive compassion.

Honor your words, so your words will be honored. Love what you say, so your words are taken with love. We do not see what we do wrong in our actions. Yet, in every direction of us, something can be improved. Learn to speak how you feel and provide an explanation of your thoughts. Open up completely; not just halfway. Look in their eyes, so they see the meaning of your words. Speak slowly with meaning, so less confusion arises. If they do not understand, find ways to help them understand. Do not get mad because of misunderstanding or miscommunication, it won't help. Helping others understand your thoughts allows you to communicate better and helps them to see what they are doing more clearly.

When speaking to others, try not to sound demanding. When you demand, you get resistance and tension arises. When you ask with kindness, they are more willing to accept and honor your request. Treat your request with appreciation and treat the person with gratitude. No matter what your request is requiring, treat it with respect. Ask in a manner that you would want to be asked. Do not make someone feel less of a person by your ungratefulness and attitude. Treat them with importance. Meaning, speak with clarity and respect. Do not speak as though others are there to serve you, rather speak to establish equality. Do for others the way you wish to be treated yourself; nothing less and with no excuses for wrong treatment.

Speak with reason rather than ridicule; not only to others but first and foremost to yourself. Focus one hundred percent of your energy to the positive messages you speak. It is always better to give than to receive, so give more and expect less in return. However, if you are in need of help, ask and you shall receive. Let others be there for you with love and not just because they are your wife, friend, or family. Treat them with love so it will be returned to you for the right reasons and not the wrong. Give all you know how to give and not what you feel like giving. Learn to cherish life and not to dislike life. Be inspiring and not negative. Do not just take sides with a friend, be encouraging to the situation. Do not speak badly about someone behind their back and then treat them different in their presence. Change you as a whole, not just in certain areas. Help others in the right way instead of helping someone make it worse by agreeing with their wrong treatment or comments. Learn to support instead of running away. Learn to be strong instead of weak. Be comforting, reassuring, and positive;

do not teach someone to be cold and uncaring. You can teach goodness and love with strength, without telling them to walk away.

Dig deep inside yourself in search of the information and answers you wish to seek. This information will begin to unfold on your journey and help you see areas that you would have not thought existed from within. To see what you were blinded by, ask your angels for help and the signs will begin to appear. They will show you something that is so easy to see, but would have been so difficult to find on your own. Guidance from the angels makes your journey bright and beautiful. The angels help you understand where you need to find the changes within, when you are thinking of the good and bad. They help you see faster and help with the changes you need to make within yourself. For example, when you see your wife, friend, or family member upset, do not get mad at their tears or emotions. Those tears are there for a reason and not for show. By getting mad at the tears, you are getting mad at their emotion and self-expression. Your anger will only bring more hurt, which will bring more tears. This goes for men and women, because men get upset as well. Learn to face others' feelings with love and comfort. Learn to heal and not destroy. Learn to comfort, not ignore. Learn to address instead of take flight. As you can see there are many ways to improve ourselves. If you look at this right, you will feel the comfort and not the negative actions. You will start feeling the freedom of the misery you are living. You will see the glory of happiness and be grateful that your destiny is written out for you and it stems from within. Just remember it takes time to learn and understand how others receive your messages. So be patient, speak with love and continue your journey with more understanding and respect for others. Keep trying with every word you speak.

Learn to live from within your heart and not your mind. Teach by showing good and not just speaking it. Teach love by giving love and not just saying it. Give all of who you are all the time and not just occasionally. Remember to love and treat yourself good while you do the same for others. Do good for yourself in an unselfish way. By doing this, you come across stronger and with respect. Makes sense, doesn't it? It is hard not to speak with anger. When you are in the heat of the moment, speak with passion. They will understand you are upset. However, they will reply with respect as well. Do not think this is not true, for the fact you have not done it enough to find out. As you will learn, speaking with honesty comes more naturally because of the results you receive. Also, when something upsets you, wait until the right moment to discuss your feelings. There are many reasons in doing so:

1. You are more in control of your emotions.
2. Your intentions will be for the right reasons.
3. There is a perfect time and place for everything.
4. Allow more time to internalize situations and resolve from the love within.

Time also allows us to learn how to speak with more comfort and you start learning how to leverage:

1. Tone
2. Ease
3. Caring
4. Appropriateness

An important note to remember: when you are in a disagreement, have a valid point along with reasons to back your position. Don't just say something to disagree. Explain in detail why you feel so strongly.

In doing this, others might understand your position and agree with you rather than trying to read a closed book. Both parties might learn something in the end result. Arguments do not mean one person is right. We've all heard the saying, 'There are two sides to every story,' but this is not correct. There are no stories involved; there are only feelings and emotions to be considered. The saying comes across as if one person is to blame and that is not true at all. It means two people took things in different ways and had varying reactions. So the saying should not be used because it is hurtful. Other people's feelings are involved here, and both have their past reflecting on how they respond to each situation. Each person will look at the situation in their own perspective. So no one is wrong on how they feel, just misunderstood in how to respond properly within a dispute. Paying attention to one another's reactions and talking to each other properly will help resolve the matter more effectively. It's also important not to take sides when offering an outside perspective.

Many relationships dissolve because of not understanding each other intimately and it typically causes miscommunication between one another. This in turn can easily lead to turmoil and hurt. We need to learn how to understand one another.

Listen to who you are speaking with and do not cut them off in conversation. Listen to what they have to say and then respond; as you expect them to listen to you without interruptions. There is a need for respect in this life and it seems we only give it with limited reasons. We need to learn to give respect so we can expect to receive it in return. Learn to give respect to everyone you come across every day, even if you do not know them. If they are rude, teach them not to be or let them know it is not necessary. You can teach people how to react with kindness in the right manner. By doing this, you are respecting yourself, and you receive it from others. Remember, do this with an effective and appropriate tone. We speak every day without thinking how important this is in our daily lives. We need to understand that we hurt others without even knowing it and that this is one of the ways we hurt people without the knowledge of this action. In acknowledging this act, you will begin to see why there is so much hurt existing within our everyday lives. We've been walking this earth with our blinders on and it's time to take the blindfold off and see what role we play in this life of hurt.

Accomplishments Regarding Part Four

Accomplishments Regarding Part Four

Accomplishments Regarding Part Four

Accomplishments Regarding Part Four

Accomplishments Regarding Part Four

Accomplishments Regarding Part Four

Accomplishments Regarding Part Four

Accomplishments Regarding Part Four

Accomplishments Regarding Part Four

Accomplishments Regarding Part Four

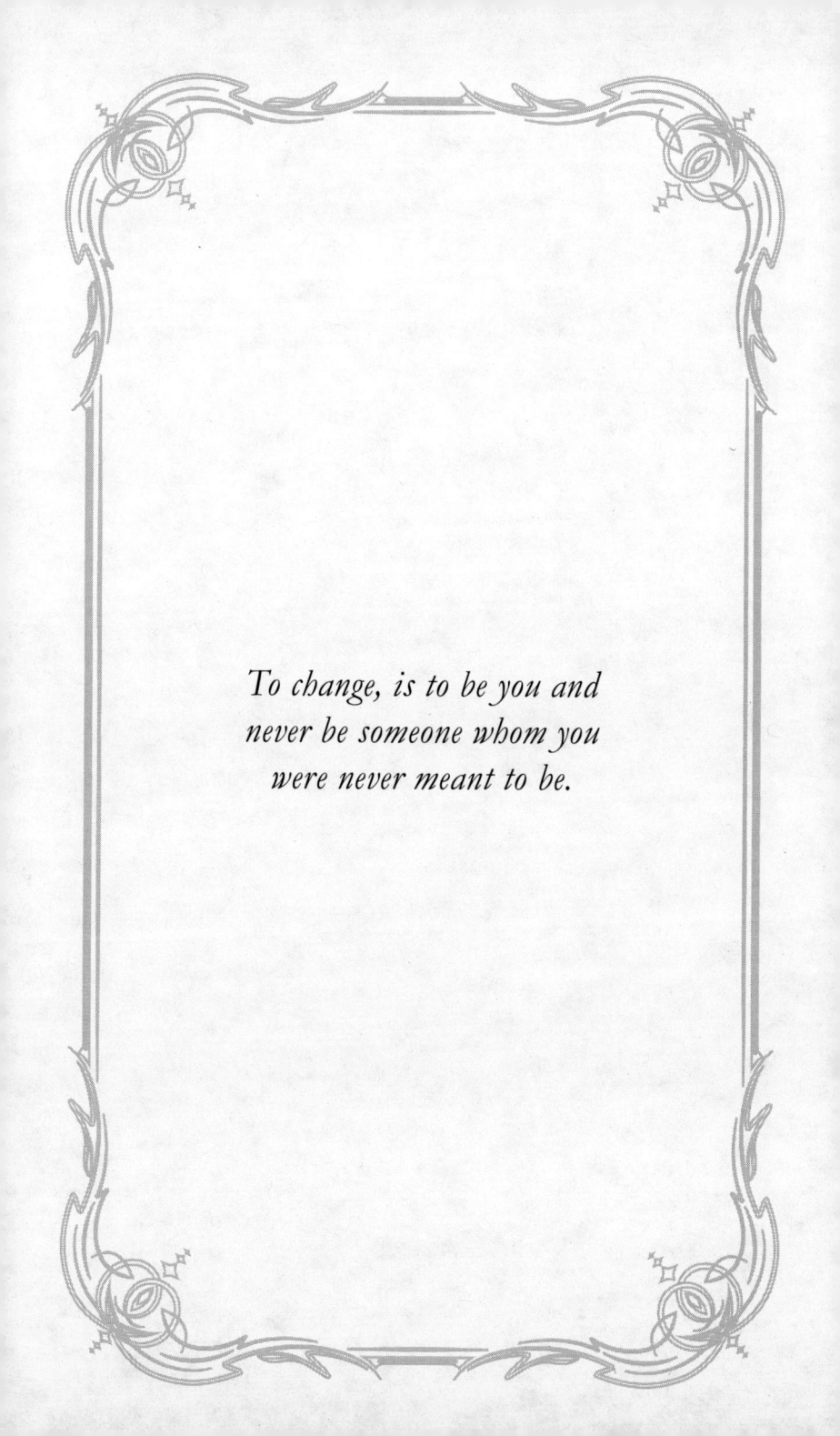

To change, is to be you and never be someone whom you were never meant to be.

Part Five

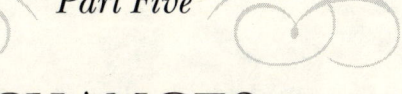

CHANGES

So far, you have learned about the situations in your life that have not been included in your everyday thoughts, prayers, and focus. The angels, as you can see, can help you realize the changes you need to make within you. Believing in their messages and guidance can help you make your changes faster and easier. This life is a beautiful one and the angels want to help you love yourself the way that you need to be loved. Here are five simple rules to loving yourself and others.

1. Be kind.
2. Think of others.
3. Speak with love and with honesty.
4. Listen to others with their feelings in mind.
5. Speak about your feelings without trying to win a discussion.

One of the many challenges we face in disagreements is we think someone has to win, instead of the understanding we can come to an agreement. We think someone has to be wrong, instead of seeing both might have a valid point for the better. We are too busy trying to see who is right and who is wrong, instead of resolving the situation. Does this make sense to you? Ask yourself if you've ever perceived a disagreement in this way. If you have, great, but how often do you apply it? And if you have not, it's okay, be happy, as this is yet another direction you'll need to go on your journey.

Angels do not point fingers to make you feel that you are wrong. They help you see how you can become complete with yourself. The days of your journey can be full of different emotions: happiness, sadness, anger and so on... The important thing to remember is that as your days go by the love of your angels stay with you, on your journey of life. It is only the days of life that go away; the love always stays within you.

Now let's get back to the disagreements. Think of how you handled them in the heat of the moment. Did you get mad and walk away, only to return like nothing ever happened? Did you come back and apologize for getting mad and not listening to the other person's feelings in the situation? Or did you sit down and explain why you got mad and apologized for your actions?

Think about the various responses and how you can react in the future. Then ask yourself, which response would be the most effective and a kind-hearted way to understand each other. By doing this, you will release the anger and frustration that lives within you. In addition, you have more respect for each others' feelings. You will also establish a higher and deeper understanding of each other. This applies with all relationships, not just intimate ones. When you learn to speak appropriately to one another you don't carry so many burdens. You begin to feel the stress being lifted off your shoulders and begin loving with greater passion.

How you handle your life and the choices you make is what brings the weight you carry. Whether you realize it or not, you are getting guidance on how to change your life and become divine. You're learning new ways to look at who you are and how to gain control of your life, instead of life controlling you. So, take the gift of life and make it the gift that was given to you with love and happiness, with honesty and health, and with caring and understanding. Let go of the hate, cruelty, and selfishness. Continue thinking about which one you truly want; a life of happiness or a life of loneliness. We all yearn for love and we all want to give love. Did you ever consider that this is why we have anger inside? It's because we have not received love the way we are truly meant to receive it. By learning this you'll make the best investment you ever made: love yourself with honesty, integrity, and understanding.

Learn to be there for others the way you always wanted someone to be there for you. The angels will help you in all directions. Just ask them to show you the direction you need to take. They will provide signs much like at a crossroad; you'll know which one you need to take. Take these situations and signs and work on them. Be happy that they are showing you the way; do not be mad at the situations and most importantly do not run from them. Do not walk out on a confrontation or a situation.

Take what you have learned and fix the issue at hand.

Now let's move to the same subject of a disagreement, but in a different direction. Picture yourself in the middle of the disagreement; you're angry. Are you yelling and screaming, or are you speaking calmly and with true emotion and feelings? Some of the most painful occurrences in disagreements can be name calling, direct attacks and lashing out from internal anger. Name calling to hurt someone because you are mad about the situation is uncalled for. Cuss words are demeaning, painful, and can even scar a friendship, relationship, or family member beyond recognition. Words such as, "You're stupid," "You don't know what you're talking about," "You're dumb," and last but not least, "I don't care," can be devastating to someone. Think about how you felt when those words we're said to you in a disagreement. How did those words make you feel? Or are you the only one in the disagreement that makes those comments? Think about it for a minute. Does the other person put you down in the heat of the moment? Or are they just upset stating their emotions? Mean words do not help whatsoever and they just intensify the disagreement to hurt and cause pain.

Name calling leaves little scars that echo in our subconscious mind that need time to heal. These are negative actions that are done out of anger to try to win an argument. Do not try to find a winner and a loser of who is right and who is wrong. That is not the purpose of a disagreement. It just means that there is a breakdown in the communication, or in one's actions. Think of the cruel words you speak as little daggers that cause internal bleeding to you and to others. They hurt deeply and cause damage to many lives. Do not put people down; this dilutes respect from yourself and the way people look at you. Guaranteed, it is not wise or worth it. Especially to people you love. It can or will weaken your relationship. Is the relationship worth it to you? Does the victory mean more to you? Think of the pros and cons: are you truly winning or losing? Are you losing feelings, happiness, and love or even losing them period? Think again: are you winning the situation from uttering those cruel words or actually losing?

Stop the hatefulness and be the better person if it truly matters. Sooner or later those words take a hold on the relationship. Maybe not in one instance, but can little-by-little break the structure of the relationship until it crumbles. Everything you do will reflect in your life. In this step of your journey, learn to think before you speak. Do not destroy the people that matter to you by your mistakes and negative actions. You only end up suffering with regret, and sometimes it can take a lifetime to try to heal.

It is hard to change your life, but that is why you never give up trying. It gets easier along the way; however, your continuous efforts should never stop. The more you try, the greater your life and who you become will magnify beyond your wildest dreams. Learn to expand your mind and resolve your anger in the difficult moments; do not just take the beaten path. Use the strength of your soul and mind and ask your angels for guidance. You can achieve anything when your focus is on your desires. Don't stop practicing; practice every day. Envision your every move and learn to watch yourself more than you watch others. Learn to face yourself, when you know you have done wrong. By doing this step it will help you face others' wrong doings. Do not hate yourself for your mistakes, just learn from them and keep walking your journey. As I have mentioned before, this journey is not easy. However, you can get through the hardships by knowing your angels are there to help you change and to help you see between right and wrong.

The more you work on your downfalls and face yourself, the faster you get through them. Remember, do this with love for yourself, so you may love others the way you want to be loved. When you know you are doing wrong, Stop! Just stop right then and there. Make your climb to the height of your spiritual summit shorter, instead of longer. It is easier to fix when you learn to stop hurting someone when you know you are hurting them.

Change your habits and make them righteous instead of trying to win a situation. Learn to win with yourself and the rewards will benefit for you and the people in your life. Learn to compliment them, in place of telling them what they do wrong. You can tell them the good as well as the wrongdoings. Think about it: How often do you complain about them and compare it to how often you tell the good? Do you make others feel special or do you judge their every move? Do you look at them in how they make you mad or do you look at them on how they compliment you? Do you have a better understanding of all that is involved? Again, time is everything. Learn how time can benefit you on your journey: how time is your friend, even when it seems to be against you.

Time is on your side. Make time a good thing and do not use it as an excuse. Do not use time against you, use time as a healer. Accept your wrong doings and try not to blame other people for your hurtful actions. Don't get mad at them because of what you've done. They have the right to be mad. Do not get angrier because they are mad at your actions. Face what you did, and hear what others have to say. Take time and listen so you can learn of others and the hurt you caused. Do not act like others should suppress their feelings to benefit your ego. Do not tell them not to feel their true emotions. It is what they are feeling and we should all be more accepting of them. Do not act cold to others if you love them. Show them you care by acknowledging their emotions and reciprocate by actions of love. Remembering all of this is difficult, that is why there are these steps in place. They are all small parts of your journey, but lead to your success.

Important note: Do not read this book and then *not* take action or make the effort. Do what the angels guide you to do with your journey. It will change your life. Do not just read books of enlightenment and think, "What a wonderful book," but then *not* act on the information you have learned. You will not get anywhere by doing nothing with this knowledge. When you take action, you have the right to say you are trying. Practice what you are learning with all the strength you have. When your life is calm, that does not mean you should stop trying because your life seems easier. Try every moment of your life. Take your responsibilities seriously and take control of you. Do not let anger, power and cruelty control you. When you do this, your life will take a negative turn, but at least now you will understand why. When it does, do something about it. Get back on track and keep walking with strength and courage.

Accomplishments Regarding Part Five

Accomplishments Regarding Part Five

Accomplishments Regarding Part Five

Accomplishments Regarding Part Five

Accomplishments Regarding Part Five

Accomplishments Regarding Part Five

Accomplishments Regarding Part Five

Accomplishments Regarding Part Five

Accomplishments Regarding Part Five

Accomplishments Regarding Part Five

*Actions can be deadly or
actions may be joy.*

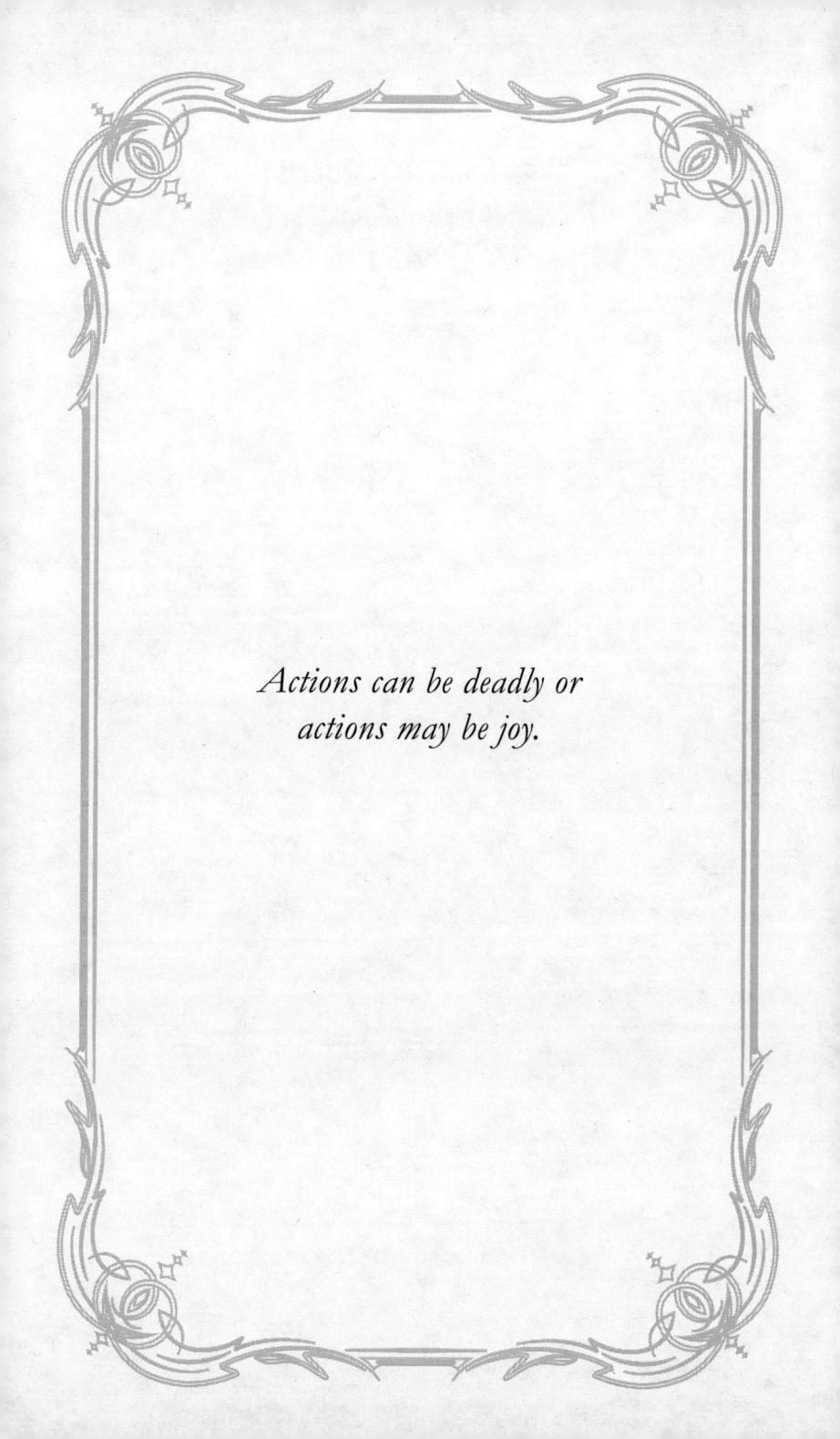

Part Six

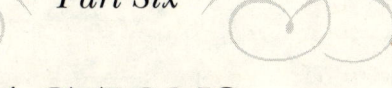

ACTIONS

Your actions are a true reflection of the pain or joy you hold in your life. The emotions you choose to share with others can and will make them feel worthless to the point of depression or raise them to the top of the highest mountains with love. You alone have the choice to make them feel hate and anger or happiness and love. Cruelty is poison that can kill anyone's happiness, yet it is usually the first emotion we choose to share. Pain is a terrible feeling to carry within, which can be one of the reasons why you are cruel to others; however, if you dislike carrying it within you then why are you so willing to inflict pain on someone else?

This is not a very happy way to live life. It also makes people live in fear. Why would you want the kind of power that makes you feel you can control someone else? In reality you don't have control over your own actions. Why would you want someone to be afraid of you, but then you say you love them? You treat people that way because of how you feel about yourself. Change your inner monologue and learn to live your life with love; instead creating a life of misery. Some of us fight so hard to keep a person's love with threats, in fear that we might lose them. When you love someone, you take care of them, protect them, support them, and show them the love you carry for them. Do not beat them down due to your struggles from within. This can bring an unrecognizable sadness to others that can be hard to face. We all visualize dreams of love and seek happiness and guidance from spiritual mentors. We all dream of love because we have the power to manifest true happiness from within before finding it externally.

We all need guidance in every direction of life in order to bring back the good. There are wonderful people that are trying to help us with this mission; people who can bring eternal happiness through their efforts. You may not think you need help on certain parts of your journey, but this guidance will allow you to understand the lesson in every step you take. Understanding the messages, information, and guidance that your angels provide you will help you unfold any doubts about your passage. The more you see, the more you understand. The less you feel of yourself, the more you take it out on others. Making the right choices in life makes you more confident of yourself. Many of you may not understand, because you have not yet ventured down this road. When you work on yourself and separate your wrong from right, you find the happiness is within you. In effect, it stays. You cannot receive eternal happiness from anyone until you realize it lives inside of you. This might not make sense to all, but it helps you get through the hardships of life.

Finding your inner strength builds a foundation for love and happiness. No one wants to live a life of heart-wrenching pain, loneliness for love, hurt or sadness. Break this chain of misery. You alone, along with your angels' guidance have the power to achieve all that you seek. The biggest challenge is believing in your inner-strength and guidance. Listen to your intuition and your passage will unfold before your eyes. Most people are unaware of their inner-strength and don't have the courage to accept change. Remember to take your time but never give up or stop trying. When you stop trying, is when you set yourself up for failure. So, don't give up!

How much do you mean to yourself? How much do your loved ones mean in your life? Have you ever wondered what your life and heart would feel if you're loved ones were not there to provide support? Why do we blame others and not accept our own downfalls? Why do we hurt instead of love with true passion? Why do we lie and refuse to say the truth? In doing this, we live on the opposite of life's true meaning.

Living a life of anger takes too much energy; you can live a life of happiness without doubt, lies, or deception. Do not walk your life pretending you know everything or acting like you do not care. We all care about our lives, so why hide it? Learning to be honest with ourselves will help find the true meaning of life and true happiness. It is very uplifting and you will learn at some point you prefer the right instead of the wrong. You will also begin to realize how hard it can be to juggle the balance between right and wrong, so just keep working on making the right choices and being honest with yourself and with others. In doing this, you can learn so much about your life and the beautiful journey ahead. Even though your journey can be difficult, it is worth every second. You don't have to be a certain age to walk this journey with the angels. Anyone can change their life at anytime. Life is hard to live, so why not take the time you have and make it a beautiful experience of love and miracles.

We all think miracles happen now and then, and they have to be big to notice them. Miracles come in all sizes. You can see them every day, if you stop to look around. We also think miracles are only good, which is true. However, when you walk your journey with the angels, issues will arise that help guide you on your journey. Miracles come in all different forms and for different reasons; many we do not understand. Miracles are used as educational tools that will help you with your transition from a life of wrong to a life of liberty. Remember, miracles are an act of God, so thank God for each and every one.

If you wish to make your world a better place to live, inspire your freewill. Freewill is the power of choice—a gift from God, but yet we use it not only against ourselves but against God. Freewill can be difficult to handle and your test of time. Are you going to use time to do right or wrong?

Freewill can and should be used for you and not against you. Why use it to make your life a world of misery? Why not use your freewill to complete your happiness, instead of taking it away? Use this gift to understand life, instead of wondering why there is a life of pain.

Accomplishments Regarding Part Six

Accomplishments Regarding Part Six

Accomplishments Regarding Part Six

Accomplishments Regarding Part Six

Accomplishments Regarding Part Six

Accomplishments Regarding Part Six

Accomplishments Regarding Part Six

Accomplishments Regarding Part Six

Accomplishments Regarding Part Six

Accomplishments Regarding Part Six

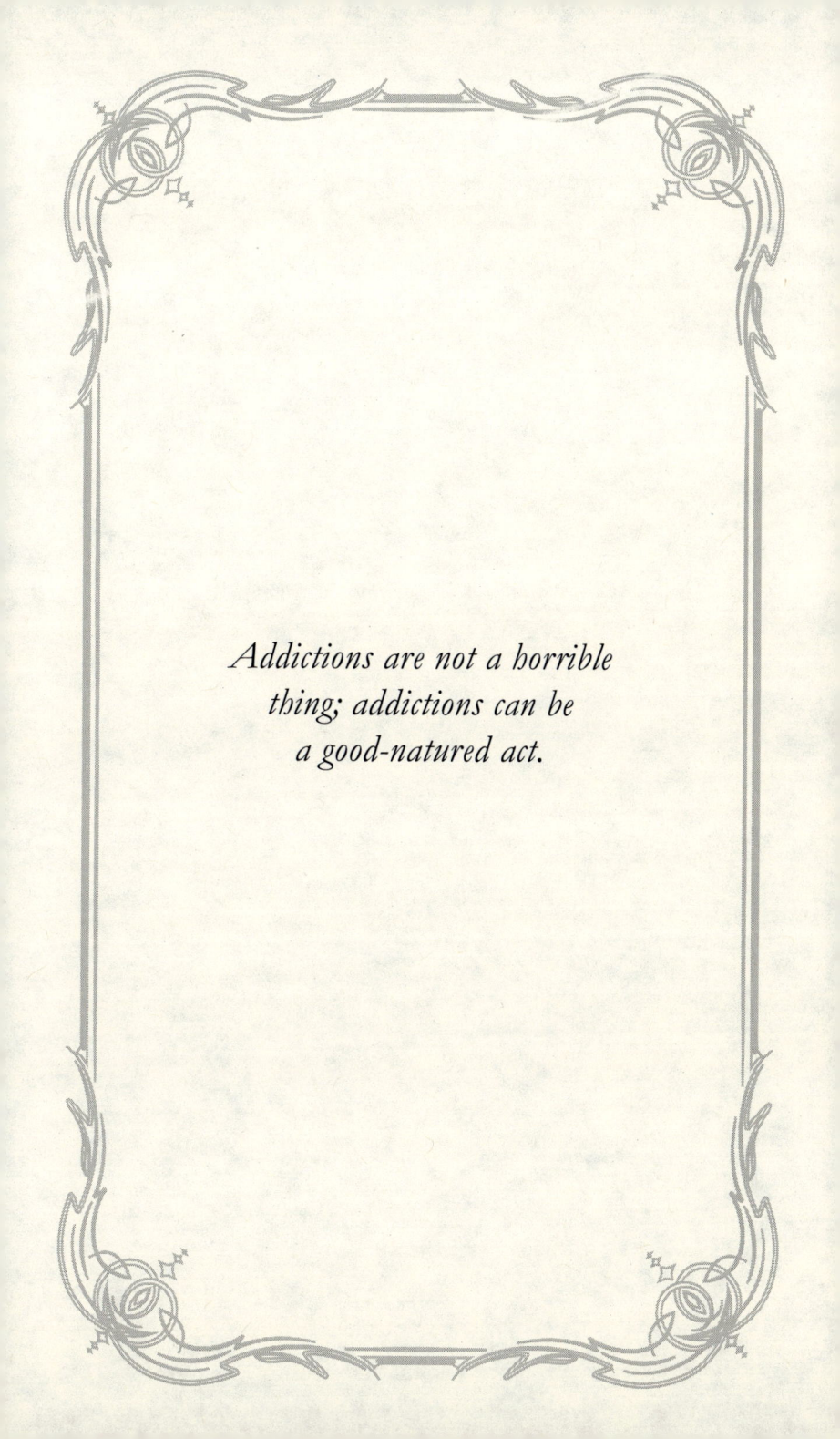

Addictions are not a horrible thing; addictions can be a good-natured act.

Part Seven

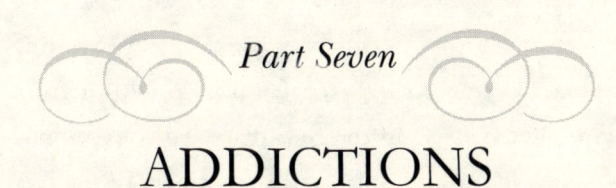

ADDICTIONS

Addictions can exist in many forms and are not only related to controlled substances. Addictions spawn from your inner habits and negative thoughts. Addictions can be a curse that destroys all that is good to you as well as to others. Addictions are a very serious matter that should not be taken lightly so pay attention and take your time to understand this section of the book.

Cruelty is one of the strongest addictions that can cause death to marriages, relationships, and can even drive a human being to inflict harm on themselves or others. Cruelty goes hand-in-hand with anger and fuels this addiction without notice. We love to be angry because it influences us to punish others. When we punish others, we release the anger of another person's wrong doing. The wrong doing was never forgotten from its origin or from who gave it to us in the first place, so we continue to take it out on the world, carrying this anger inside us for a life time. No matter who we lash out on, the anger boils inside because we never learned to heal or release the addiction. This is why cruelty is deadly and can lead to suicides many times over. The pain caused is so unbearable to others that they believe the only way to get rid of so much hurt and pain, is to take their lives. Cruelty has driven us to the point of killing ourselves because of the hurt lying dormant within. Suddenly erupting like a violent volcano—causing harm to anything in its path and taking the lives of many. Cruelty is like a poison that kills everything it touches. It is a terrible way to live life, yet it makes us feel empowered. Cruelty makes us feel like we are in control when in reality it ruins our lives because we pay the consequence of losing someone we love.

Selfishness is another addiction that can hurt just like cruelty. Only thinking of oneself can hurt other people and drive them to hold anger toward you. They begin to hate you because you only think of your needs, and not the needs of others. As the days go by it builds more and more inside of them. Being selfish is destructive and tears up others with hurt and resentment. It brings uneasy feelings and a disconnection to the relationship. Selfishness will not hold a relationship together; it is a way to not let anyone love you the way they want to be loved. Selfishness takes away your happiness and pushes people further away from their emotional properties.

Being selfish blindfolds you and does not allow you to see past yourself. Now ask yourself; 'Is thinking of myself worth it'? If the answer is yes, be prepared to live a lonely life with many people disliking who you are. It is a wonderful feeling to make someone happy. I know, for this is my mission to bring back happiness in the world; to take the pain and hurt that overcomes this world and bring back the love and happiness that lives within all of us. I will devote my life doing this mission; however, it will be worth it and this is why I am here.

Anger is an addiction that we don't wish to have. However, we hold on to it because it helps us let go of where it came from in the first place. Anger is often used for power and to win a situation. The more anger; the more power we have to win. But, we actually set ourselves up for loss. The horrible emotions that rule this world are terrible. To have anger instead of love is a tragedy especially when chosen to win a situation rather than showing compassion toward the pain that's caused. The anger connects with the cruelty, which connects with the selfishness that makes our life so unhappy; yet we're not willing to change this for happiness. This is a stubborn position to hold and with little gratification in return. Why is it that we would rather win the loss, than to triumph the happiness? Anger takes hold and controls your life without even realizing it.

Have you ever thought about how often you're able to control your anger? Not many can say they do it successfully. Think about this: 'Why would anybody pick pain over happiness'? We all want happiness and not misery. Misery hurts too much and we all try and rid the feeling that eats us up inside. Misery equals depression which can also become an addiction. We run from it, even when we are the ones causing the misery. Learn to turn your addictions to self-appreciation and integrity through honesty. This journey of honesty will bring many of your wishes and desires to reality. So, continue your journey and do not stop walking. Face your fears with action and know that happiness awaits you. Remember, keep asking the angels to help you continue walking on what can be a lonely journey of unimaginable feats. Don't forget that they know everything about you, so just keep going on your journey.

There is a right and wrong with any addiction. Be selfish in the right way; treat yourself right and your wrong doings will fade. Do this with love for you so you can embrace this feeling. Stop the hurt and pain you give, not only to yourself but also to others. No one is perfect, but you can start by making the right choices in life to conquer happiness. It is easy to disbelieve that we can hurt people and not know that we have caused them pain. The hard part is recognizing it and apologizing for our actions. This is much better than doing hurt purposely or not accepting fault. However, it is much harder to say we're sorry and fix issues than to walk away and cause more pain to ourselves and others.

We need to learn to be a little more aware of how we treat others. So look at this in a positive manner, instead of getting mad because others are upset. All actions lead to a learning experience; whether or not we choose to accept them is the choice of freewill. Addictions can be overcome by applying your learning experiences within rather than immediately pointing the fingers at others. I'm not saying that all addictions apply to you; however, you know the ones that plague you. Understand this is a learning curve on how to accept your addictions and challenge your fears with positive actions.

Drug addictions are also very hard to beat; however, it does not mean that it is impossible. Having a strong position and an understanding that you have an addiction will allow you to conquer it head on. There are many opportunities to give yourself everything you need to overcome this situation, including: placing yourself in rehab, listening to friends, and accepting the guidance and signs from your angels. Learn to take care of yourself in a loving way, so you can share that love with others. You have to be in control of your mind in order to win this personal mission of yours. Don't let your addiction control your mind or your outcome; conquer the substance with the desire to be free.

Do not be afraid to face the battle of drugs and addiction. The beginning may seem like a positive shift in the right direction but will challenge your will when you get the urge for a fix. It's not the drugs or the addiction that you're battling, it's the inner pain and hatred that drives you to abuse drugs, friends, and loved ones.

What is it that you're trying to ignore and don't want to acknowledge? Why do you quickly accept defeat and choose drugs, instead of seeing life for what it truly is? What is it that is so bad that you choose drugs over friends in order to get through these issues? Would you rather be high on life's happiness or high on drugs as life passes you by? Give yourself the help and the support you need. Your family and true friends will be there for you (not the friends you do drugs with). All you have to do is make the first step with yourself and then ask your family and friends for their love and support. Tell them what you need from them. Let them know you want to change your life. Tell them you want to be happy and to learn to treat them right. Let them know you are tired of lying to everyone, hoping you do not get caught in the next lie.

Lies do the same damage as other additions. They tear up your life and the people around you. Think to yourself and ask these important questions: *Do I want to act like I don't care that I am unhappy'? 'Do I want people that I love to look down on me, when all I truly want is for them to be happy and proud of who I am?* Remember, when reading these questions to yourself, that this is between God, his angels, and you. They know the true answer, which lives inside you.

Take your journey all the way. Don't just do what you want to do. Do not pick and choose what you have the strength to deal with. Take all of it and do everything possible to change your life. Work on your addictions and throw them out of your life. Do it with your soul, work hard and strong with determination. Pick you; choose a life of less pain. Do every thing you can to heal your pain and release it from your soul. Do not let your soul be a storage room for hurt, pain and abuse. Move your hurt and pain out and move in peace. Live your life with true meaning. Time will heal your soul; however, it needs your help. Time cannot take all your hurt away by itself. It just eases it, so you need to help get rid of it completely.

Why would you want to carry hurt in the first place? We seem to let hurt take over our hearts, which in turn takes over us. We cover ourselves with depression because of the mistreatment we've received; especially from someone who at one point in our lives expressed love and affection. Addictions of cruelty and the addiction to win ruins not only your life but the ones you love. The abusers carry the hurt and others carry the consequence of our actions. So give up the addiction, the excuses, and the pain, and seek the life you've always wanted.

Break the cycle of addiction with love and understanding so you may walk toward happiness and allow others to love you again. You can start by accepting the fact that you might fail once or twice but rise victoriously with a new found glory: love. By doing this, you can take away the pain that you inflicted in others so they can heal as well. You are one of God's children and he will help you on your journey. He will bring you happiness, so you can better your life. However, God will also help with bringing back the misery, when that is what you are giving.

Accomplishments Regarding Part Seven

Accomplishments Regarding Part Seven

Accomplishments Regarding Part Seven

Accomplishments Regarding Part Seven

Accomplishments Regarding Part Seven

Accomplishments Regarding Part Seven

Accomplishments Regarding Part Seven

Accomplishments Regarding Part Seven

Accomplishments Regarding Part Seven

Accomplishments Regarding Part Seven

*Messages tell you everything,
all you have to do is read.*

Part Eight

MESSAGES

Have you ever wondered why you have some of the dreams you have? Did you ever consider that some of your dreams could be messages to you? When your loved ones' have passed away and are in your dreams, do you ever wonder if it is really them coming to you in your dreams? Not all dreams have meaning, but there are reasons for why you have them. It could be that they are sending messages to get you to think in nonlinear ways. It could be a medium for your loved ones' that have passed to talk to you without scaring you. Dreams can also give you directions and messages in your life, including how to overcome fears. Yet, we discard our dreams and do not think about them much, unless they really get to us or scare us.

Do you ever ask God or the angels to give you a message in your dreams before you go to sleep? If not, you should try asking your loved ones' to come and talk to you and to help you with your journey. Now when you do this and it does not happen that night, don't give up asking. They do come at the right time and tell you what you need to hear. They will give you messages and talk to you about your life. This will get your attention when it occurs, so do not question whether it was real or not—especially when you have been asking for their help for quite some time and may not have even noticed the messages you've received. Even if you do not ask for the angels' help during your journey, they will come and help you.

Everything happens in synchronicity or divine timing. Even if you don't think it was perfect timing at that moment, you will eventually see how time plays a key role in your journey. You will begin to see the reasons why things come to those at perfect times, and you will learn to be grateful for them. Once you learn to pay attention and understand these messages, you will be amazed by your answered prayers and by the simple law of attraction. The more you believe in something the more likely you will receive it. The more evil and negativity that you feed on the more it will feed on you.

It can be hard to walk this life without understanding why we are here, yet many people choose to walk blindly. However, the people that choose to remove the blindfold soon realize that this is hell and the evil that walks this earth, feeds on anger which fuels the fire tenfold. We are the evil here on earth and we alone write the table of contents for the chapters that lie ahead. We need to unite in harmony to change the hate and anger into love and forgiveness. We need to start from within and work outward toward those who need it most. We all want peace back on this earth and joining together will make a world of difference. We need to invest this love into the hearts of others so we can reach as many people as possible so they can pay it forward.

Your journey with the angels, will be a beautiful experience. It will change your life completely; not just in some areas, all areas. You will see this more and more as you walk with the angels down this heavenly path. You will fall in love with the brightness you feel inside. You will feel an overpowering sensation when you start to feed on the respect you feel for yourself. You will learn to care for yourself and who you are becoming. You will learn exactly how it feels to start loving yourself the way you only dreamed others could do. Your morals and values will become even more apparent of what is right and wrong and it will matter to you. Walking this journey not only opens some doors, it can open all doors. There are many of us who see this change as a closed door, but are afraid of walking through it. Whether you accept it or not your angels are standing by you looking through the door, holding your hand, and wanting to help you walk through that doorway with you. Once you begin to see this, not as a challenge or as closed door, but as an open door, it will be easier to walk through many more changes.

Learn to uphold your morals and values, such as: honesty, love, truth, caring, understanding, listening, friendship, family, life, and inner self-respect. There are so many ways to uphold morals and values. Take honesty for example, it can bring so many outcomes depending on how you use or abuse it. Try to take one week without being dishonest with yourself or other people. Take one week with without accepting the wrong over the right. You will see the positive differences and miraculous outcomes within that week. Do this for the right reasons, as we all know, life is to difficult to live for the wrong. Not being true to your life will only make life worse and full of misery. It may not be miserable all the time, but enough to wish you had more honesty in your life. Be good to yourself as only you have the key to unlocking true happiness. No one can do it for you or take the wrong and make it right. The decision is yours. We need to understand and see the evil in what we do, so we can see the evil that walks among us. When you begin to truly see your surroundings, you will understand why this world is falling apart and how you can help rebuild the love and peace that waits.

Why is it that we do not care about ourselves enough to try and make the effort to change from within before trying to change what is around us? Why do we not have the courage to be kind and loving? Why can't we give unconditional love rather than expect to receive it? A love that helps the ones' you love in your life. A love that doesn't just say, *I give up;* but an unconditional love that will stand up and fight to bring back the harmony in life and in your relationships. Why has it become so hard to show love completely toward our wives, husbands, children, coworkers, and friends?

Why can't we hold someone when they are in need of a hug? Is it because you are mad and love is not worth fixing the issue at hand? Is being mad more fulfilling? Why do we fear closed doors when we know a better life is calling, urging us to push forward? Why is love so hard, when love is supposed to be coupled with happiness? When loving, why is there unbearable pain and hurt involved, when there should be gleaming eyes and a glowing smile? Why is love a tragedy, instead of a reward? It is truly sad how easily we give up love because of an argument or a position of anger that can be fixed by understanding and forgiveness. We need to make love a reason to fight for not against. We need to learn to make arguments a beautiful experience of understanding, instead of a painful feeling of regret.

We are so afraid to feel new emotions. We don't pray to God to help us survive our own destruction or even pray to God when we're happy. We don't talk to him all the time, yet only when we are suffering and in need of him. We can't accept that God is there all the time and not just some of the time. We look up when we speak to him, when he is right here beside us and within us. He said, "To love one another as he loves us," yet we don't even try. Could it be because a lot of this world does not even think how much he loves us? We walk around this earth only using part of our souls and giving even less back. We do this because we are afraid of what would happen to us if we used all of our soul and love.

Why do we dwell over our mistakes rather than accept and forgive ourselves from our own actions that we've done to the people we love? Is it easier not to apologize or is it because you do not have the strength to deal with your own personal damage? Learn to live for your happiness in the right way, so everyone around you feels the happiness too. Understand the brightness inside of you is in your control. You have total control over the switch that shines the amount of light you hold. If a light switch was a metaphor for your happiness, wouldn't you want it all the way up? Or would you rather turn the light off and live a life of misery?

Don't let fear ruin your life and control your mind. Let life be beautiful, let your journey take flight instead of a putting up a fight. Be happy and be loved. Fight for the good and do not give up on love. For, love is life and it is up to you when to live it.

Accomplishments Regarding Part Eight

Accomplishments Regarding Part Eight

Accomplishments Regarding Part Eight

Accomplishments Regarding Part Eight

Accomplishments Regarding Part Eight

Accomplishments Regarding Part Eight

Accomplishments Regarding Part Eight

Accomplishments Regarding Part Eight

Accomplishments Regarding Part Eight

Accomplishments Regarding Part Eight

*Your journey is your life,
so trust in your steps.*

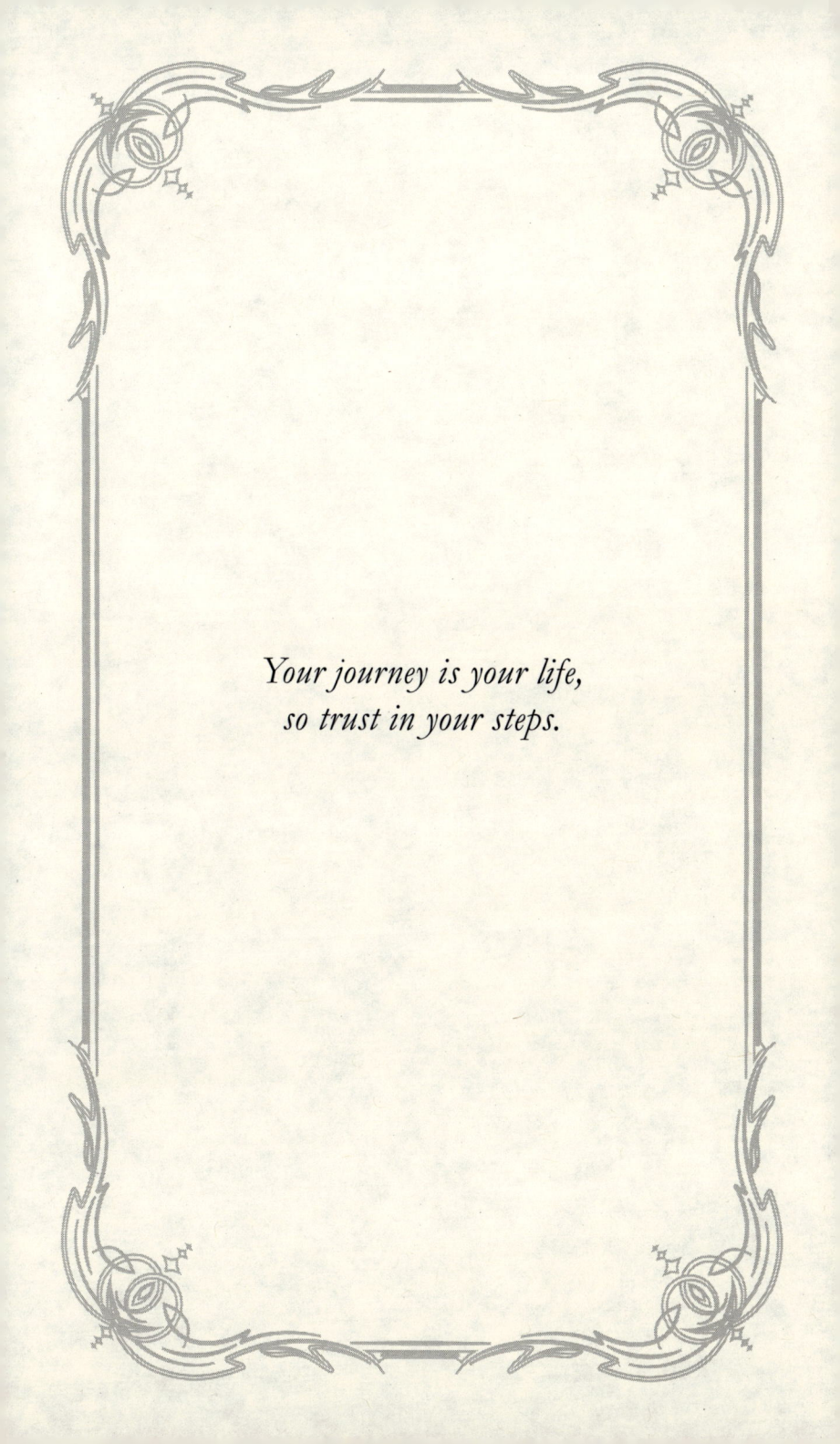

Part Nine

JOURNEYS

Journeys are an experience of love, chance, forgiveness, change and the strength to push through the anger, frustration and self doubt. Journeys are life's lessons many times over. Take your journey with all your love and strength that is hidden within you so that you can feel the doors open for more love. Take this time for you, whether you are alone or not. Take this journey to open your closed doors. Take this journey knowing you are changing your life. Trust, believe and know it will be hard, however have faith in yourself that you can get through those moments. Know that hard times will come to you, but not harm you. Know that love will conquer and not destroy.

Be all of you when walking this road of change, so that you can transform this doubt into self belief. Believe in yourself and believe in God. Let life be good to you, instead of being afraid of life. Learn to live. Learn not to be lost with the ones' you love; learn to be lost without them. Learn to miss them when you are with them, and don't wait until they are gone. Learn to reach out to them when they are in your life and don't wait until you are wishing you had when they are not. Learn to give and not to take. Learn to trust and not to accuse with doubt. Learn to ask, instead of expect. Learn to speak truth, in place of lies. Learn to be who you are meant to be. Learn to believe in yourself and learn to let others believe in you too. Learn to listen and not just to be heard. Learn to accept, instead of turning your head. Learn to be happy with God all the time and not just when you need him. Learn to pray to him in place of getting mad at him, for he is only teaching you where your life is going.

Learn to laugh more, instead of cry more. Learn to wipe away others' tears, and not cause them. It sounds so simple, but we aren't realizing what we are causing, instead of what we should be empathizing. Let's bring happiness and stop the harm. Let's walk this journey with courage, to endure your life without excuses of why not too. Learn to talk about the feelings you feel inside and act on them. They are there for a reason. Meaning, that if you know it is wrong, don't do it. Do what is right. Trust in yourself with love for you. Be good and you will receive good all around you.

Life is meant for reasons we may never know, but that is not a reason to make it harder for others for things we do not understand. Just because we don't know the true reasons why we are here, does not mean we should destroy this gift given to us. This journey can help you enjoy what has been given to you. It will help you see that it is a gift of love, and learn what love is all about. Live with love in our soul, and feel the pain of love, so we may learn to treat love right.

Do you ever wonder if love is the reason why we are here? If you really think about it, isn't that what life is all about? Everything connects to the end result of love. Love is the reason we are here and yet we play love like a game of ping pong; hitting our hearts back and fourth to no remorse. It's a sad conclusion when our fear drowns the love we long to receive and give in return.

Take the help from your angels and learn to love fully and learn the pain of love. The pain helps us learn what love is about and who we truly are inside. It helps us learn what we need in someone and to see the good and bad in people. It helps us to see what we do not want to become and who we want to be. This is why we should not be afraid of the hurt when it comes to opening our hearts. We know we can learn something from the experience and/or find the treasures we have been seeking. Instead of tearing people down by throwing faults in their face, we should be making them feel special and let them know that they are meaningful in our lives. We need to stop walking around this life scared. Know the angels will not let harm come to you, especially when it is not your time to pass. Live your life with them, so you feel their protection. Do not live just knowing everyone has angels.

Talk to your angels with all your fears, worries, and even the good in your life. They love when we walk our journey of life hand-in-hand with them. So, take hold of them; you will be amazed what you see and learn by their messages. Seeing all their messages brings a comfort and serenity to your soul. You'll see the energy, and know it is them and/or your loved ones, not just a chill in the air. You can feel them touch your shoulder, hold your hand, place a hand on your knee, or just standing by your side. It can be a little scary for some at first, but you will learn to embrace the touch. You can even see them, but again some of us, not all, just think to ourselves that we really didn't see anything and it was just our imagination. I can tell you it is not.

Know when you hear them—it is your loved ones. You will not hear your angels; you will only get their response through their messages, and let me tell you, they like to talk. You will see your life in a completely different way. You will love the comfort that comes from them knowing they are with you. Learn to talk to them throughout your day. The more you talk to them, the more you see their messages. You will smile at what you see. You will sigh with relief. You will laugh many times over for the fact you are happy and receiving their messages. You will love it more and more each day. You will start looking forward to your days, instead of dreading them. You start to build a relationship with the angels and feel the relationship get stronger and stronger. The nice thing is that you learn that you have angels that you can trust. The beautiful moment is when you know that you can tell them everything and it won't leak out and it will stay private. You start loving them and holding on to them; it's no longer just the angels holding on to you.

You will learn to understand that they hear your prayers and that you can count on them. You know they won't hurt you, and they will be there for you when issues arise. Walk this beautiful journey with them and change you from the inside out. It is so beautiful to have angels from heaven living your life with you. You will never feel alone through the hard times or pain ever again. You can talk to them in all situations knowing the angels will take care of you on your path of change.

It is a scary realization; however, you will learn that you just need to keep walking with them no matter how hard it gets. Then, watch the beautiful outcome. Give the angels your love and learn what pure love is supposed to be. You feel safe with them. You feel that you are loved in the right way. You feel that you have someone on your side in life. They help bring you the light and take away the darkness. They help you succeed on your journey throughout your whole life. So let's take that journey of life, and learn where we are going, and not worry where we will end up.

Walk this journey with eyes wide open and not half shut. Learn to look all around your journey and not just look straight ahead. Don't worry about what is at the end of the road because life is about the journey not the final destination. So, walk this life knowing there is not an ending to your journey because your journey does not come to an end. The only thing that comes to an end is the evil, not the journey. The journey keeps going and going.

God is trying to talk to you. God already knows what our lives were going to be, but with freewill, we create more of the wrong and he is trying to tell us to live the right. Hear him. Do not turn away from what he is trying to tell you. If you are addicted to drugs and losing everything, don't you think that he is telling you to stop and go get help? You can receive this message before everything is gone. And, if you do lose everything, do something to get it back. You can fight in the right way, and you might get it all back, right away. However, this is where you let time in and do not stop fighting. Speak with truth and love. Tell all what you have learned and how it has affected you, and time will move a little faster. There are such things as a second and third chance. Not always, but that is where you give it to God; if it was meant to be, it will be.

Pray with your soul and not just for what you want. Pray with feeling, love, and meaning in your words. Do not use your words just to get what you need. If, or when, your prayers are answered, do not forget your words of hope. Do not only have faith when you allow yourself to have it; have it all the time. Do not put God's time on your schedule; put your time on his. Do your journey with the angels with serious intentions and not with the thought, "I will give it a try." When the first hard lesson comes, don't give up and say, "I am not doing this anymore." You might as well keep walking with the angels and try to keep changing for the better. For that reason, just because you give up, the situation does not go away. Keep walking, see the beauty, and don't only see the bad. We always seem to look at the bad and not the good of why things happen. We look at life so wrong, which is really hard to watch. To me, I have a hard time seeing it, because I know what it could be: less crime, happier people, and not so many of us walking around with a scared heart. You can talk to God anywhere; you do not have to go to church to talk to him. He knows where your heart stands. Do you ever just sit in your room, put a pillow on the floor, light a candle, and have a conversation between you and him? You will feel comfort, relief, and feel better when you take the time to have a conversation with God.

Accomplishments Regarding Part Nine

Accomplishments Regarding Part Nine

Accomplishments Regarding Part Nine

Accomplishments Regarding Part Nine

Accomplishments Regarding Part Nine

Accomplishments Regarding Part Nine

Accomplishments Regarding Part Nine

Accomplishments Regarding Part Nine

Accomplishments Regarding Part Nine

Accomplishments Regarding Part Nine

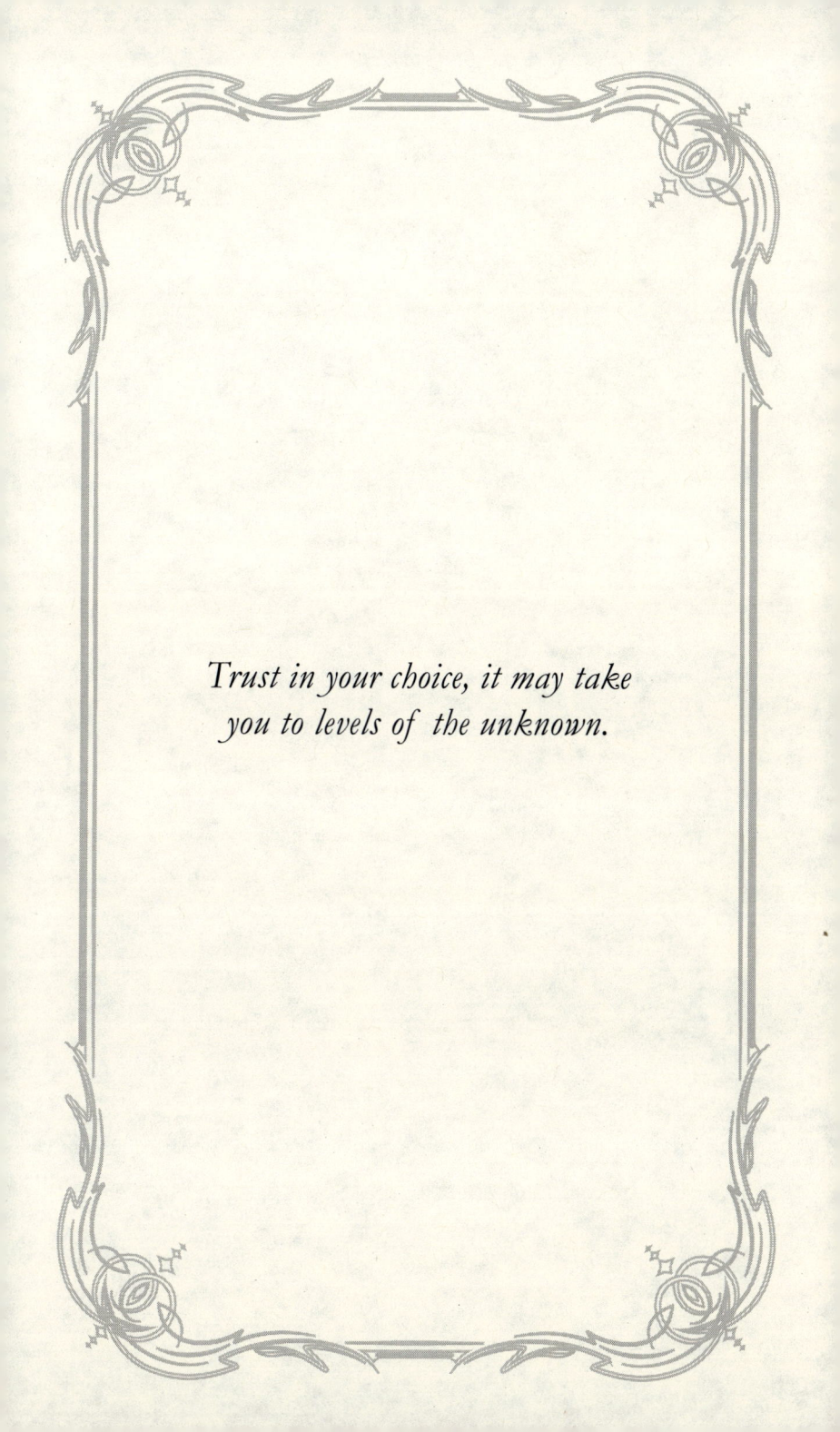

Trust in your choice, it may take you to levels of the unknown.

Part Ten

MAKING A CHOICE

Who are we inside? Who would we rather be? Would we rather be happy or unhappy? We all go through hard times. Instead of living our lives with bad habits, why don't we learn to stop our cruelty and "turn our lives around" and go the other direction? Life has more meaning and understanding when you take a deeper look inside yourself. It is amazing what four words "turn our lives around," mean and how they can alter the direction of our lives. When you truly learn the depths of written words and how deep they really can go, then you will start to know more about you, and who you really are inside. You will like some of you, and will see what you want to change.

There is nothing wrong at all with reintroducing yourself to you. It is a nice way to get to know you and who you really are as God intended you to be. You have to be able to understand you, your change, as well as trust your intuition. Intuition is there for a reason, but very seldom used for its intention; guidance to the right choices in life. Intuition is that gut feeling telling you something, and a lot of the time we do not listen to what it is telling us. Intuition can even save your life and save a lot of wrong choices we make. That feeling is telling you something and guiding you in the right direction. The angels speak to you and can help you to understand the right and wrong. If something does not feel right, it is probably because it is not a good situation. Give it a try and see in time why you had that gut feeling inside. Time is needed to see most answers, but you will see them more when listening to your intuition. At times, you can see the results in seconds, sometimes it is days, and sometimes it takes weeks. We need to learn to watch for the reasons of that gut feeling. Then, you realize why it's important to trust your intuition and the reasons for the events that take place. Do not just focus only on your outside life; focus on your inner voice and intuition.

We work hard to move up in our jobs and get what we want on the outside, yet "What do we do for our inner peace"? We need to turn it around; focus your attention inwards and the rewards for the outside come more frequently. You will realize you are doing the right thing and you will not have to try so hard for the outside accomplishments; they will begin to come to you. We give ourselves a chance in many ways on the outside, but do not do it for the inside. We give encouragement to others and very little in return to ourselves. Take time to think inward, not in a selfish way but with an inner peace and understanding of harmony from your soul. Make this promise to yourself and not just to others. Think about that statement for a minute.

How many times have you given someone a promise and kept the promise; now, how many times have you given yourself a promise and kept the promise to you? Think about when you kept that promise to someone else and how good it felt. Now think of how good it would feel to promise yourself to change and to keep that promise no matter how many times you wanted to give up. How does it feel to keep your word when it comes to you, not just your reputation to others? Have you ever given yourself that chance?

Think of your life like a metaphor for building a house. Would you give up when you've laid the foundation and just begun to build the interior structure? With all the time and effort you have put in building your house, would you just let it stand there and get ruined? Most likely your answer should be no. You would keep building your house until the very last tile was laid and until you know you have accomplished inner peace. Live in your peace for years to come and do not let the work you have prospered stand there and get ruined.

Be proud of your accomplishments and cherish it, just like you would in your new home. Live there forever; make it homely with the changes you keep making or with the changes you have made. Make your home as beautiful and elegant as you can imagine, for you are the one living in your home. If you do not like the home you are living in now, rebuild your home. You will never run out of maternal love to make it more livable. Where you live is your choice. Think about that... Would you rather live in a house that is falling apart or would you want to live in a well built house? Do you want green grass or dead grass? Do you want flowers or weeds? Do you want a house with no lights on and no one home or do you want a house full of energy and light? Do you want a house that people want to go inside and look around or just drive by feeling sorry for the person who lives there? Imagine how much money it would cost to build this house. Now think of how much it would cost to change your mindset and find inner peace.

Maintain your new home with love for yourself and respect for your hard work. Keep working on your new home to keep it as beautiful as you've made it? It's wonderful to be looked up to and not walked away from. It is incredible for someone to want to see more of the inside and not close the door behind them. You are your home and have to live with yourself. So how do you want to live? Let your days teach you the lessons of life but look for the signs of what you are learning through your mind, body and spirit. Be grateful for the days ahead and look without anger or fear. Let your *Days Go By, Not Love*.

Learn to take the anger and replace it with insight. Learn to accept change instead of close the door and walk away. Learn to love each day and not wait until that day goes by. You alone have the power to make the choice, the choice of enlightenment or the choice of sorrow. Think about how strong those five words are, "You alone have the power." You learn to feel good with the people you have in your life because they admire you for who you are and not what you have. What people have cannot help you, but who they are can. Move from your old house into the new, and get rid of the bad neighbors who bring you into despair. Just remember, it takes time to get to know your new neighbors that come into your life. If you don't like the area where you live, move to another. You have the power of who is in your life. You have the power to keep them there or to be honest with them and tell them that is not your way of life.

Allow the positive and not the negative in your life. You have the power of your every move, thought and action to create positive outcomes. You also have the power to not have the power; meaning you can give up the freedom of choice. Do you want the negative to power your new home or the positive to take care of your new life? What do you want? Give yourself the power to make the right decision. You have the power to give yourself strength and you have the power to take it away. You have the power to do what is right and the power to do wrong. You have power to give hurt and the power to take hurt away. You have the power to run and the power to prevail. You have the power to be happy inside.

Do you want your relationships to succeed or do you not care if you lose the person you love? Do you want people to side with you or do you want to receive the truth? There is so much to think about on your journey, yet it is easy to overlook. That is why your journey will be so inspiring to you when you begin to believe in the unseen. The insight and the knowledge you receive is so beautiful and it can grow with you if you feed it with the positive and not the negative. Just continue walking and you will feel the changes you're accepting for yourself. The journey is remarkable and you will start loving instead of dreading it in every step you take. Your journey does not change who you are inside it only brings out the true inner peace that has always been within you.

There is so much to think about, don't you agree? However, our lives are worth it. Just try to take it one day at a time, write in your journal and you will begin to see your life change through your continued efforts. Do this with every attempt to accomplish this change, not just when it's convenient. It is hard to stop your habits and addictions; however, you can if you do not give your power away. Remember, when we fail ourselves, we fail others. Everything has an impact on our lives. When we do not have trust for ourselves, it is difficult to trust others. Why scar, when we can help heal? Why destroy, when we can build?

Never forget that your angels are walking with you every step of your journey. Talk to them as if they are a friend you visit often. Knowing they are there through the good and the bad times, while you are watching TV, and even in the shower. Yes, everywhere you go and everything you do, the angels are with you. You are being watched since the time of birth. Take this journey whether you walk, run or just stand there. Walk with them, for they walk with you.

This journey is hard to endure, but in the end happiness awaits. Hard at times to take, but take because of love from within. Be there with every direction with pure intense love. Never walk away and to never let go of their hands. For that is your strength to walk through to true happiness.

Take this journey for love within yourself, for you. Take this journey with the angels, so that you can reach happiness, for you. Reach for your hopes and dreams and take hold of them. Even if you do not know what they are, you will find them along the way. Love is one of the many hopes and dreams; however, beware of how you treat it when you have your dream. Some wonder how they lost their dreams somewhere along the way, and maybe to some, it is because of their wrong doings. It could be to teach a lesson in life, or a sign that will take them down the right path later in life. From these lessons, we learn of our own needs, and learn how to give others theirs. We learn how to think of others' feelings and not just our own.

When you love yourself, you don't have doubts if you're worth being loved. You begin to understand the good within you and you do everything in your power to treat others with true love. This understanding brings a realization that you are just as important as the one's you share your love with. Love is not to be tested, it is to be reciprocated, nurtured, and enjoyed with endless happiness between all that share its beauty.

Never stop learning or following the signs that your angels put forth in front of you. Remember to be honest with yourself during this journey, as it is easy to steer ourselves onto the wrong path. Learn from your mistakes and turn them into lessons of love and forgiveness against those who trespass against you. God created all men equal, but he also gave us the gift of freewill. So learn to love others how you want to be loved. Show them how you want to be loved, and how you can love them in return. Walk in the light of love, instead of the dark. Let life lead the way, instead of you leading your life; live life from the soul and not with your mind.

Let this guidance help you see so you can walk in a positive light. Let life be an experience and not a punishment. Let your passion for life live with you and your loved ones, not live dead within you. Let life shine hope and not sorrow. Let life bring you strength and not weakness. Let life be magical and not mystical. Let life teach, instead of fail.

When you turn your life around from sorrow to sunlight, you also turn how you handle the hardships around. Be good to yourself and share your happiness and self acceptance with others. Let people love you and let them understand you. They can understand you when you speak to them of your journey, and share what you are learning. You never know, you might help them begin their journey. Open up and let people know what you are doing for you and your life. Let them see that you want to change for the better. They will be inspired by what you have to say and what you are doing. If they are negative, you already know which direction to walk.

On your journey, read this book over and over. Read, read, and read, so you will remember where you are walking and why. Use it as encouragement and strength. Let this help you to keep walking to your dreams. Do not lend this book out; however, give one as a gift, so they may do the same. Take this book and make your house a home. Remember, do you want to own your home or rent? Do you want your home to be treated with respect or treated with disrespect? Do you want others to treat your house with care, or do you not care if they walk in your home and break what you've worked so hard for? Meaning: do you want someone to come in your life and break your heart, emotions, and your confidence? Take back the ownership and control of your life and your happiness. Don't give someone the power to tear your house down. Think of you in the right way and look at what you are grateful for in your life. Continue with the good you have and throw out the bad.

When you love your soul from within the place you live; the lights will always be on, the family will always be home, and the happiness will always be shared. Love yourself for the good you have and the dreams you want to share. Learning how to improve yourself and become who you truly are will bring out all in which you desire. Learn to appreciate you and let go of the fear. Learn to be thankful to yourself for making the right choice for you and your life. Learn that life can be good and so can your outcomes.

Learn and be happy that you have made a simple decision, yet for some it may be the hardest one to make. Live your life with love, so you may be loved. Learn to be you, and be happy with what you find. Know that you will still make mistakes, but learn to forgive yourself knowing you learned from them and you are not giving up. Learn that life is hard and will get easier as you grow and continue on your journey.

Love God and your angels. Know they are there for you with the purest love one person can receive. Take their love and trust in them. Walk our journey with peace and strength. Walk with the promise to yourself and promise of success. Trust in your steps of change for your happiness is waiting.

Accomplishments Regarding Part Ten

Accomplishments Regarding Part Ten

Accomplishments Regarding Part Ten

Accomplishments Regarding Part Ten

Accomplishments Regarding Part Ten

Accomplishments Regarding Part Ten

Accomplishments Regarding Part Ten

Accomplishments Regarding Part Ten

Accomplishments Regarding Part Ten

Accomplishments Regarding Part Ten

LETTER FROM THE EDITOR

I'd like to start this letter with one of the teachings from this book about making a promise to yourself. "How many times have you given someone a promise and kept the promise; now, how many times have you given yourself a promise and kept the promise to you? Think about when you kept that promise to someone else and how good it felt. Now think of how good it would feel to promise yourself to change and to keep that promise no matter how many times you wanted to give up."

When I met Therese, I was walking blindly (among many) in a field of doubt and despair, with many unseen barriers to the answers of the questions I had long been seeking. Some of the biggest and most complex questions that had always challenged me were, "What is my life purpose," and "Why am I here?" And, had I not met Therese, I would have been continuing to seek the knowing yet unknowing divine answer that had been given to each of us since the days of our birth: love.

From the moment I met Therese, she opened my heart and reached inside my soul; reintroducing the fiery passion of a love I once felt for myself and for those around me; a love that I chose to close the door on because of a deep hurt and pain I was secretly enduring within. And during this reintroduction with this love, it reminded me of a promise that I had made to myself, over and over, as a young boy. A promise to help change the world, to help release the pain, and bring back the warmth of love to those in need.

Therese has shown me in her methods of teaching how to see love in all situations and in ways that I would have never thought possible. Her teachings help us remove the blindfold and comprehend the true understanding of love and caring about people in ways that show our every day actions of love are misguided by our own freewill.

So in writing this letter, I ask you to challenge your freewill. Make a promise to yourself to change for the better. If you've already made a promise to yourself; keep it and continue fighting for its freedom. Choose the right over wrong and watch the miracles unfold to bring a warm and loving light into your journey. Let your love shine through as love conquers all fear.

—Jason Benedict
Editor

AUTHOR'S NOTE

To all who have read this book of change, may you climb the highest mountains and soar among the heavenly clouds. May you breathe with peace from your journey and keep taking your steps to happiness.

To be you is to be all of you. Never let yourself down, but forgive yourself as you grow. Do not beat yourself up while you walk your journey. Acknowledge your mistakes and learn from them and keep walking to be all of you and not part of you. Love you as you walk this life of wonder and learn who you really are and why you are here. Trust in yourself, for you hold the key to your life. Be patient with yourself and let yourself have the time you need to learn and the time to overcome. Love you everyday and let the Days Go By, Not Love.

ABOUT THE AUTHOR

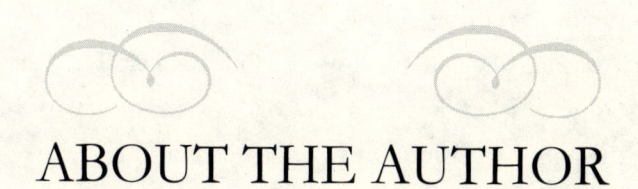

Therese Benedict is a clairvoyant with an undeniable gift, which allows an authentic and direct communication with God and his angels. Throughout every moment of her life, Therese works endlessly with the angelic realm to bring love, peace, and healing of past and present to help change one's life from wrong to right. Therese communicates with God and his angels through many divine channels including seeing, speaking, hearing and through physical and spiritual healing. This book is written in God's words to help people learn how to think, act, and start changing their lives to love and to forgive themselves of their past and present actions and to help them change those actions to beauty. Therese was presented the *Congressman's Metal of Merit* by Congressmen Steven Schiff for her countless acts of helping the community of Albuquerque, New Mexico. Having survived and healed from Melanoma Cancer, Therese continues on her mission of healing the world through her vision, knowledge, teachings and most importantly; love.

Contact Therese:

yourjourney_1@yahoo.com

or

http://theresebenedict.tatepublishing.net